SEEING THROUGH THE DARKNESS

SEEING THROUGH THE DARKNESS

The Incredible Story of How Losing My Sight Taught Me To See

LAURIE DEVERNOE

Foreword by Matthew Medick

SEEING THROUGH THE DARKNESS
THE INCREDIBLE STORY OF HOW LOSING MY SIGHT TAUGHT ME TO SEE
© 2024 Laurie Devernoe

Published by Laurie Devernoe | Troy, NY
ISBN (Print): 978-1-7379976-2-7
ISBN (Kindle): 978-1-7379976-3-4
Library of Congress Control Number (LCCN): 2024903310
Printed in the United States of America
Cover Design by Onward Marketing
First Round Edits by Michaela Decker-Lawrence
Manuscript Edit by Wendy K. Walters | www.wendykwalters.com
Prepared for Publication by: www.palmtreeproductions.com

To contact the author: www.lauriedevernoe.com

To my fellow sojourners
whose suffering has changed how they see

SEEING THROUGH THE DARKNESS

ACKNOWLEDGEMENTS

To my husband, the strongest man of faith I know—you always bring my focus back to Jesus. I could not have survived a moment of this journey without you.

To our kids, Rachael, Rebecca, Sarah, Ronnie, and Caleb—you suffered alongside me and stood alongside Daddy in faith to make sure I didn't surrender to the darkness.

To my surgeons, Dr. Eden, Dr. Schutlze, and the Cornea Consultants staff—I felt like Norm walking into Cheers; through tears, laughter, and disappointments, you never gave up your unwavering support.

Dr. Huz, Dr. Walsh, and Dr. Pokabla—your compassion and dedication to your patients and craft shined in every appointment. Dr. Grill—you completed my team with love and understanding.

To each person who whispered a prayer, who stormed the gates of heaven with prayer, made a meal, offered an encouraging word, and sent voice memos for me to listen to—you have no idea how much strength you brought me.

And to those who said I would write about the journey even as it began to unfold—you planted a seed, and God made sure it grew.

To Angela—you reminded me how God still speaks through dreams. Every one of you shined your light and helped me find my way through the darkness.

SEEING THROUGH THE DARKNESS

PRAISE FOR SEEING THROUGH THE DARKNESS

Seeing Through the Darkness is a story of discovering deeper faith than she thought possible and exploring the goodness of God even when you don't yet have the answers. Laurie Devernoe is a true warrior who walks in grace as she forges ahead, experiencing everything God has for her with the trust of a child, surrendering to His timing.

JOAN HUNTER
Author, Evangelist, Host of *Miracles Happen* | www.joanhunter.org

Laurie's words are paramount for anyone who may be suffering, knows someone who is suffering, and who is having a hard time reconciling their faith with the problem of suffering. She bravely and passionately shares her story in a way that brings hope to the reader. Laurie is a wealth of wisdom, and she doesn't cut corners when it comes to the reality of pain. She is raw and honest about the darkness, but her words, rooted in biblical truth, bring light to see the next step. Everyone should read this book because everyone goes through hard times.

JENNIFER CHENOWETH
Worship Leader, Pastor, Mental Health Advocate

In this heartwarming real-life journey, Laurie shares intimately how God developed her inner strength to overcome obstacles as she walked in ever-increasing faith that will impact your heart.

You will be drawn into this story and discover the reality that God is truly good and that His love is unconditional no matter what circumstances you may encounter. As Laurie shows us, this does not mean God gives you what you want, but He gives what you dearly long for in your heart-of-hearts—His presence—where we encounter His unconditional love.

That's the heart of our heavenly Father, and on our journey, we discover this life is not just about "me." Rather, it is about walking as a beloved son or daughter surrendered to His goodness and love no matter what our circumstances. Here, we are at peace, content in being Father's beloved child. Laurie's story will help us discover that our life circumstances or challenges do not define us, but through God's grace and the exercise of our faith, we grow in our true identity as Father God's dearly loved child.

STEPHEN P. LALOR
MSW, LCSW, MDiv, Ph.D

Seeing Through the Darkness is a personal journey that brings to light how faith is lived out. Laurie unveils that when our expectations may be limited in the natural, God brings our expectations to see what He is doing in the spirit realm around us. Allow the Lord to pull back the veil of hurts, disappointments, and brokenness as you read so you can gain spiritual eyes to see and allow healing to begin!

NIKKI TEBBANO
Wife, Mom, Friend

Pastoral Assistant at Harvest Church, Women's Ministry, Front Line Youth Minister

In her poignant memoir, *Seeing Through the Darkness*, Laurie Devernoe bravely shares her journey of faith amidst the shroud of adversity. As someone whose unwavering devotion to God was met with unforeseen challenges, Laurie's story resonates with authenticity and raw emotion. Through the loss of her vision in one eye and the absence of the miracles she fervently prayed for, Laurie confronts the depths of her faith and emerges with newfound clarity.

Laurie's willingness to navigate through doubt and disappointment with vulnerability is truly inspiring. By sharing her life message, she offers readers a unique opportunity to delve into their own relationships with God. Through her struggles, Laurie provides a roadmap for readers to confront the complexities of trust and belief within their own hearts.

Seeing Through the Darkness is a testament to the unyielding presence of God in the midst of life's darkest moments. Laurie's profound insights birthed during a season of faltering faith remind us that even in the depths of despair and tangible darkness, God's light shines brightest. I wholeheartedly recommend this transformative book to anyone seeking reassurance of God's faithfulness and the enduring power of hope.

DEBBIE DUFEK
Author of *Holy Interruptions: When God Taps You on the Shoulder*
Podcaster of The Women Behind the Words
Inspirational Speaker & Storyteller, Certified Writer and Speaker Coach

Seeing Through the Darkness does not shy away from the hard questions—the impossible questions. With a lifetime of cookie-cutter religious answers and formulas that failed her, Laurie Devernoe's memoir grapples with the tension of God's goodness and the reality of present suffering. With raw emotion and unvarnished self-exploration, Laurie pushes through the darkness and, at last, finds clear vision of the One who has captured her heart and holds her in His tender, loving, perfect care.

WENDY K. WALTERS

Author, Editor, and Ghostwriter | www.wendykwalters.com

CONTENTS

F O R EWORD

"Consider it pure joy when you come into various trials!"[1] I had no idea what that verse meant the first time I read it, but I found myself in the middle of what would be a five-year-long trial—mostly of my own making. I began by declaring by faith, JOY, in the midst of my trial. Whenever something would go wrong, I would say to myself and sometimes out loud, "JOY!" This, along with continued reflection on the scripture from James, led me to a deeper understanding of what that scripture meant and a joy—deep joy that is not dependent on circumstances.

When you go to read this book, do yourself a favor and set a couple of hours aside because once you start, you are not going to want to put it down. Laurie has done a masterful job of weaving together her own personal experience, with revelation from the Lord, alongside biblical application. As she shares the depth of personal trials she has gone through with open and raw thoughts and feelings, you are invited on a journey of learning how to consider it pure joy when you come into various trials of your own.

There is a certain aspect of knowing God that is only available to us as we go through trials and sufferings. As we embrace the trials and the suffering, as Laurie has and shares deeply about in her book, we come to a much fuller understanding of who God is, His great love for us, and His unchanging goodness.

As you read this book and share in Laurie's experience, allow yourself to do some personal evaluation and reflection. Is there some traumatic event you have experienced that still has a hold over your life? Are there areas of your life that you don't think you need to relinquish to God because you have it under control? Apply the lessons that Laurie walked through to your own personal struggles and trials. Draw from what Laurie has gone through and allow the words on these pages to help you see through your own darkness to the glorious light of Christ.

MATTHEW MEDICK
Lead Pastor Redeeming Love Church

ENDNOTE

1.   1. James 1:2, NKJV.

INTRODUCTION

Smoldering embers replaced the mountainscape view. The landscape, once populated by fragrant wildflowers, was now worn. The wounded warrior limped through the battlefield with half of her armor hanging off her body and the other half missing. The assault of the enemy surrounded her. "One more step, just one more step," she whispered in searing pain. Dried blood from unattended wounds and infection covered her tired frame. Broken arrows strategically embedded their way into her soul.

Shots fired in the distance, and her anxiety exploded. She searched for refuge but found only fear. She looked back to discover everything she once believed in ... now gone. Unable to take another step, she crumbled to the ground.

With just a few more days until Christmas, my to-do lists had to-do lists. Yet, this year, I honestly couldn't wait for the holidays to be over.

Don't get me wrong, I love Christmas. I'm right up there with Buddy the Elf, and I can't seem to get my fill of favorite holiday treats and events. The fast pace of life left me long overdue for time and space to let my mind and body rest. Somehow, I kept pushing on, hoping rest would come. In an effort to feel better, I planned to start a cleanse and a fast at the beginning of the new year.

Raising a family with five children kept life full with an overflowing schedule all year long. Like many others, we kept pushing on to the next season. I frequently made empty promises to myself: *When* we get through the school year, I will rest; **when** we get back to a set schedule, I will have more time; **when** I complete this busy season at work, I will take a day off.

I just kept pushing.

New Year's Day approached, and I expected the calendar change would lead me into *my year.* I had released my first book, *Coffee House Parenting,* and was working toward changing my career. A culmination of multiple facets of my life was finally falling into place. My schedule would no longer be running me, but I would be running my schedule—or so I thought.

Time to get back to my lists, I shook myself from dreaming about my future. However, my right eye began to have a little tickle. *Maybe you just need to lie down for a little bit,* I told myself.

And I did so ...

... for the next three months.

On Christmas morning, sunglasses on to shield me from the pain of light, I sat up long enough to witness my family's attempt to celebrate.

My husband tried multiple ways to find medical attention for me over the next few days. Offices were closed, urgent care centers were overbooked and understaffed, and I simply just wanted to rest on the couch, where I could hear all my people. Being around them reminded me I had to be okay. They needed me.

I started the new year in the emergency room at our area's largest medical center, about to embark on a series of medical treatments in an attempt to save my right eye.

Save my right eye ...

If they were attempting to save my right eye, that meant there was the possibility that I could lose my right eye. I could not even reconcile the thought.

But ahead of me were more medical treatments and procedures than I could count, all in the effort to restore my vision.

I did not yet comprehend how losing my vision in my right eye would commission me to see ...

... to see in the darkness.

EVERYTHING HAS
ITS WONDERS,
EVEN DARKNESS
AND SILENCE ...

—HELEN KELLER

C H A PTER 1

HELP MY UNBELIEF

*"Faith is when you stop believing what you see,
and start seeing what you believe."*
— K A T H R Y N   K U H L M A N

The warrior lay on the ground surrounded by dust. *Where am I?* she wondered, then a sharp pain focused her mind, and a moment of clarity settled upon her. She struggled to breathe. Too weak to defend herself and without the protection of her helmet, she lay as easy prey for the enemy, who inflicted blow upon blow to the right side of her skull.

The tickle in my eye turned into an infection, which caused my eye to swell shut. I'd been wearing soft contact lenses since middle school and had experienced minor corneal abrasions in the past. Being a contact lens user seemed to justify the means with the plethora of medical doctors I was about to meet.

PROFESSIONAL OPINION

My caregivers had to pry open my inflamed eye and apply two different kinds of eye drops every hour around the clock. The pain was excruciating. "I love your eyes," my husband always said. "You have beautiful eyes," and then he would kiss me. Once clear and bright, their pale blue-green color complementing my auburn hair, now my right eye had an opaque ulcer completely covering my cornea, and the once-white sclera framing my pupil was now obscured by inflamed red blood vessels. My eye no longer looked like an eye. It looked like something you buy in a costume store to terrorize people—it certainly terrorized me. I couldn't see anything from it.

At our first appointment, the cornea specialist demanded more testing than what I had received at the medical center. He was concerned that a severe eye infection like mine could quickly go to the brain, so he ordered more tests from more specialists and added oral antibiotics in addition to the drops.

The retina doctors performed an ultrasound of my eye but couldn't warrant the need for the antibiotic injections the cornea doctor had requested. They could see the effects of the infection

— however, it appeared to be isolated to the front of the eye, the cornea doctor's specialty. My adult kids took turns transporting me from one appointment to another, where each appointment totaled two or more hours. It was hard for my kids to see me suffering, yet they all wanted to show their support.

Even with my repetitive requests for some help with pain management, not one of the multiple doctors would give me anything. The pain throbbed relentlessly like I was being beaten on the right side of my head. I couldn't hold my head up straight as it dipped to the ride side from the weight of the pain. Pain gauges the condition of the eye, and the doctors didn't want to mask my anguish and risk missing a signal. They encouraged me to take over-the-counter pain meds for the most excruciating pain I had ever experienced.

I might as well have taken mints or candy, as it did *nothing* to help at all.

I ended the long day of back-to-back appointments with an oculoplastic surgeon who specialized in plastic and reconstructive surgery for the eyes. Instead of being greeted, my daughter and I were privy to hearing the staff complaining that a patient had come in toward the end of their work day. Once escorted to an exam room, the office Physician Assistant came in to ask questions and take notes with her back toward me. She did not engage with me as a person, not even as a patient. I was a subject. Once she seemed satisfied with her notes, she turned around, and with no compassion or empathy, she stated, "The eye will need to be removed ..."

I tried to catch my breath.

My heart skipped.

What? my mind screamed, though my mouth could not find the words. It was like in the movies when there was an explosion, and everything went into slow motion—every second of the blast slowed down for maximum impact.

She continued, "But we can have a prosthetic eye painted to match your other eye. It will be aesthetically pleasing. They are great at matching ..."

Her mouth kept moving, so I knew she was still talking, but I couldn't hear any of the words she said. I felt as if I had receded into a tunnel, and she was a hundred yards away from me.

All I heard was, "... prepare to have your eye removed ..."

All her remaining words faded. She didn't seem to notice that I was too stunned to ask any questions. She made no attempt to comfort me; there was no breaking it to me gently or offering any other options or solutions ... just a matter-of-fact recitation as if she had told me we were going to remove a mole.

Then she left the room.

The silence hung in the air, and I looked over at my adult daughter sitting across from me, and I burst into tears.

She stared back at me in disbelief. Too stunned to respond.

I had no words.

I kept my vision fixed on my daughter, realizing I needed to put on my big girl pants and get through this appointment. I wiped my tears. *You can cry later,* I told myself. The door opened. The surgeon came in with his three-piece suit and a large smile on his face, acting like he knew nothing of the information the P.A. had dropped. I can't remember anything he said, but it felt like he was avoiding the topic of eye removal. I finally asked, "Did she say what you have all been thinking, but she was the only one with the guts to say it?"

"Well," he responded, "that is why you are here. That's what we do."

I felt nauseous.

He smiled, which seemed cruel, and attempted to lighten the topic, saying, "I'm the type of doctor you don't want to have to see again."

I leaned forward in my hunched-over state, half my face swollen with the infection my body was fighting in my eye, with my pointer finger raised, "I will *never* see you again." I stood and walked out into the hallway with his staff staring at me for good measure.

Once safely in the parking lot, I gasped for air. Before I could even get the passenger door open, my tears fell unchecked. Once inside the car, the only words I managed to whisper were, "I wonder if I'll ever be able to hike again ..." and I leaned my head on the coolness of the passenger window on the cold winter day and wept.

Life leaves us hanging.

Maybe your instance looked like a cancer diagnosis, divorce papers, or a pink slip. You heard the words being spoken. You look around, feeling like they *must* be talking to someone else. You thought, "This can't be what's really happening to me right now, can it? Can someone just turn on the lights to reveal this mix-up?"

A CALL FOR PRAYER

The next twenty-four hours were critical for any chance to keep my eye, let alone have any vision restored. I wept bitterly. The life I had once known, along with all my hopes and dreams for the future, was evaporating.

At home, after a good cry together, my husband and I rallied our four adult children around us in our room, purposefully leaving out our youngest middle-school-age son. It seemed too heavy a burden for his young shoulders to bear. I sat on the bed with my husband sitting by my feet, holding my hand. My four children took different positions around the room—around me. They all knew bits and pieces of information from either having been with me at an appointment or from the family chat. Looking at the pain they couldn't hide on their faces made me forget about the pain I was in. Through tears and tissues, we discussed the information from the long day of numerous doctor appointments. We decided together to share openly, through social media and texts, how I needed prayer for the infection not to go to my brain, and so I wouldn't lose my eye.

As a believer in Jesus Christ for over 30 years, I like to pray for others—my loved ones, my church family, my fellow moms and sojourners of life. I pray for strangers, my husband's patients, my bookkeeping clients. I pray because I believe in the power of prayer. I have seen answers to prayer, and I have witnessed miracles. Yet, surprising to me, I quickly discovered I don't like being the one who needs prayer.

LORD, I BELIEVE

I believe in God's ability and His will to heal from the scriptures. I believed that God would perform a miracle and heal me when I learned I could lose my eye.

Yet ...

I found myself wrestling with my convictions—the convictions I once found comfort and confidence in. Despite how often I had witnessed answered prayers, I couldn't help but question unanswered prayers. I recalled and rehearsed countless stories of failed prayer where a loved one's life was lost, relationships broken, families shattered, and my faith fizzled out.

Oh, how I reached with everything I had to believe for a miracle without doubt or question. I searched for the faith to move God's favor in my direction.

I envisioned doctors documenting my condition as an unexplained miracle and saw myself testifying before multitudes.

Yet the next moment, I wondered if I would be able to care for my family again as the misery of doubt engulfed me.

At a time when I needed unfaltering faith for healing, a challenge unfolded before me where I didn't just question what I believed—I questioned if I believed at all.

***

The warrior lay in a broken heap on the battlefield, unsure of which pain was greater—the pain in her body or the anguish in her soul. To her surprise, one by one, fellow warriors of the faith surrounded her. They did not tend her wounds. Rather, they instinctively kept their backs to her, linking their armor one to another until she was completely encircled and protected from more attacks of the enemy.

And she lay there on the ground for days ...

***

Over the next few weeks, I had numerous appointments with the cornea surgeons and retina specialists, and they all agreed my condition showed significant improvement. My faith sputtered. A glimmer of hope. Instead of eye removal, they recommended a cornea transplant—*soon.*

I wanted a miracle. Total healing, not a transplant, but reluctantly, I agreed. Just in case my improvement ceased, I could see the logic in having the transplant surgery scheduled so it didn't become an emergency. We could always cancel.

Surgery couldn't possibly be part of God's plan.

Could it?

TIMELINES

The circumstances of life don't often work out as we demand them to, whether we are placing demands on God or others. Babies don't conceive at the time we expect them, the love of our life doesn't walk in at the time we map out, and God doesn't perform miracles according to a surgical schedule.

I had experience with trying to dictate a timeline for what I wanted. A crisis embedded in my family in prior years. We lived on high alert when two of my triplet daughters were in and out of the hospital with an undiagnosed bleeding disorder.

We did all we knew to do for our teenage daughters. We prayed, researched the inconclusive results, traveled for answers, and fought for a second opinion at Boston Children's Hospital. Every visit was documented, and every phone call was logged in. I bounced back and forth like a ping pong ball, from relying on doctors to provide answers to things I couldn't understand to crying out to God to heal my daughters from their suffering. The girls would hemorrhage without warning, and in dire circumstances, we rushed them repeatedly to the medical center for blood transfusions. I shook my fists, pleaded in fear, and wondered why they, so young, so innocent, had to endure the intensity of such hardship. I had an inner conflict of being angry and confused at the circumstances and took my anger and confusion not only out on God, but assigned it to Him. One moment, I would cry out to God for their healing, and the next, blame Him for not healing them.

We were left without a diagnosis after a two-year journey. We succumbed to various trials with medications in an effort to keep the girls from frequent blood transfusions. I quit my pursuit towards finding answers and laid down the battle with my faith in defeat.

Fast-forward to five years later, and here I sat with my own health crisis and the familiarity of my anxious heart beating wildly in my chest. As the date for the cornea transplant approached, I started the preoperative testing while waiting for divine intervention to manifest in some way to keep me from my fear of surgery.

Pre-op tests discovered my ridiculously high blood pressure. This was not exactly a miracle of any sort, *but maybe it was my way out of surgery?* In the meantime, I started taking blood pressure medication and was cleared for surgery.

Not the miracle I had hoped for.

The improvements I had previously experienced with my eye ceased. My condition worsened, and the scheduled cornea transplant now became urgent. Recovery consisted of a cocktail of beta blockers and, eventually, valium. *Shouldn't we have started with the valium?* I wondered.

BROKEN FAITH

My faith didn't work. I was devastated. I didn't want to answer any calls or texts. I didn't want to talk about it.

The twenty-four-hour postoperative appointment offered freedom from bandages and some cutbacks on the eye drop schedule while the familiar bondage of defeat permeated my soul.

After surgery, the intense pain began to decrease ever so slightly. I took this as a sure sign of recovery.

My surgeons examined my eye through a list lamp—the microscope you put your head into, allowing them to see a hyper-magnified view—at the eight-day post-op appointment. They told me that some of my sutures had come loose, and my eye had opened. So, they sent me back to the medical center to be prepped for emergency surgery.

My daughter and I arrived at the E.R. and were quickly escorted in. We faced another roller coaster with high blood pressure despite being on medication. So, I was given more beta blockers and additional medications, and after a three-hour emergency surgery, I was rolled into recovery.

I needed a miracle. The current state of my faith felt more uncertain than ever, and as my heart reached out for something—anything—the Holy Spirit brought to my remembrance a story in the Bible of someone who recognized the frailty of their own faith when they stood before Jesus.

"LORD, I BELIEVE—HELP MY UNBELIEF!"[1]

A father stood before Jesus, seeking help for his son, whom demons had tormented since he was a child. He was not really sure if Jesus could help his son. Two disciples had prayed for the boy earlier, but nothing had changed. The boy experienced uncontrolled moments, like seizures, where he would fall to the ground, flailing wildly with foam coming out of his mouth. Sometimes, the child would attempt to throw himself into fire or water, threatening his own safety. Anguished and ashamed, the father knew a demonic spirit controlled his son, and he desperately desired for someone to deliver his son from the torment.

Desperately desired. Hoped beyond hope.

I wonder how many times this father sought help for his boy.

How many times did he trust the counsel of others?

How many sleepless nights?

How many unanswered questions?

Standing before Jesus, the father decided to put more faith in the One he now sought help from instead of his past experience.

The man asked Jesus, "*If You can do anything, have compassion on us and help us.*"

Jesus looked at the man, compassion in his eyes, and said, "What do you mean, 'if I can?' Anything is possible if a person believes."[2]

"Immediately, the father of the child cried out and said with tears, 'Lord, I believe; help my unbelief!'"[3]

Every disappointment.

Every failed attempt.

Every broken promise.

Every missed opportunity.

Encompassed in those three words—Help. My. Unbelief.

Scripture tells us Jesus cast the spirits out of the boy, which made such a great display on their exit that those around thought the boy was dead.[4]

"But Jesus stooped down, gently took his hand, and raised him up to his feet, and he stood there completely set free!"[5]

Jesus did not condemn the boy's father for his unbelief.

When the man confessed his unbelief, Jesus responded with a miracle.

I want to be like the father who carried his son to Jesus, willing to step away from disappointment to bring the fragments of his faith to the one who heals.

Difficult circumstances become defining moments in our timelines, but these moments don't have to define us or defeat us. Depending on how we respond, the devastation life invites us to can instead become an opportunity to

DIFFICULT CIRCUMSTANCES BECOME DEFINING MOMENTS IN OUR TIMELINES, BUT THESE MOMENTS DON'T HAVE TO DEFINE US OR DEFEAT US.

discover our faith and a course of action to use our faith in the ordinary day-to-day of our lives.

Active faith, the place where the mundane intersects with divinity, creating the extraordinary.

ENDNOTES

1. See Mark 9:17-29 for the biblical account.
2. Mark 9:23, NLT.
3. Mark 9:24, NKJV.
4. Mark 9:25-26, NKJV.
5. Mark 9:27, TPT.

PART
1

THE INVITATION

C H A P T E R 2

THE STORM OF ANXIETY

"The beginning of anxiety is the end of faith,
and the beginning of true faith is the end of anxiety."
— G E O R G E   M Ü L L E R

The dawn of each new day became my invitation to crowd out my plaguing nighttime torment. In the darkness, anxiety invaded.

~~~

For as long as I can remember, I could reason my way out of an anxiety attack. In my earliest childhood memories, I analyzed life to determine the worst outcome. I claimed success when only one thing went wrong on a given day or outing. Daily life, vacations, school events, concerts, you name it—I scrutinized everything. That is until I discovered I could quiet my anxious thoughts with street drugs and alcohol.

My parents' divorce left my mom broken and alone to raise me. She welcomed my strong personality to make decisions. I wasn't qualified to make adult decisions, but I did so daily. And like many other experiences, for better or for worse, this equipped me to solve life's problems.

Life became more of a reality to me upon graduating from high school. My grandfather lost his battle with cancer, and I actively helped my grandmother run their family business. I matured and found I couldn't always fight anxiety with substances because my responsibilities held greater weight. During college, my faith became more of a priority. Some local young adults I knew started going to the same church one of my aunts attended, so I started going, too. I stopped drinking, settled into my studies, worked, and enjoyed reading and studying the Bible. I found my anxiety *manageable*.

After college, I married and became a mom, the what-ifs of life were no longer about me but now directed toward my husband and four babies. In eighteen months, I became a mom of triplets plus one, and in the chaos of responsibilities and the weight of all those little ones relying on me, my thoughts would overwhelm me. I refused to fall into substance abuse again. Instead, I became addicted to being busy. With four kids and eventually adding our fifth, both my husband and I were self-employed and active members of the activities our kids were involved in. I stayed constantly on the go, and I loved it. I felt valuable and affirmed in my role as mother and wife.

Those old anxious thoughts no longer consumed me, but they consistently hung around in the background, waiting to emerge. Being busy kept me from sitting in silence, where anxious thoughts could invade my consciousness. Being busy kept me strong enough to push the anxious thoughts away.

Until I wasn't.

MASTER OF THE BACKROADS

Our kids' activities, homeschool field trips, baseball, and music lessons kept me in the car for hours and hours every day. We didn't live close to anything we did. I hated wasting time sitting in traffic, so I became a master of the back roads in our tri-city area. I knew every alternate route possible.

During the two-year period of the girls being hospitalized, my mom passed away, and my husband spent close to a year on crutches. With so much happening, I didn't have time to overthink anything. I just kept going.

My husband and I would take turns at the hospital during our daughters' stays. One particular time, I waited anxiously for him to arrive so I could get home. His intentions for an early arrival were heartfelt, but his actual arrival to relieve me left me in the throes of heavy traffic when I left the medical center. Barely a block away and feeling trapped by both the traffic and the confinement of being in my nonmoving car, I called him in a panic as my outlet for the frustration. "I don't know if I'm ever going to get home with this traffic!" I exasperated.

"Just do what you always do," he replied, "take the backroads." His words calmed me enough to do exactly as he said and what I knew to do under normal circumstances.

Somehow, we made it through those years. Mostly, it was a blur of getting the kids where they needed to be, some doctor appointments mixed in with keeping sports uniforms clean, extra strings for instruments, meals made to eat in the car, church activities, and chaperoning for field trips. Endless lists and a whirl of activities. I orchestrated everything in detail and timed it to the minute.

Until one day, I couldn't do it anymore.

A tsunami of anxiety flooded without warning. I started having incidents, often while driving, and I couldn't remember how to get to the next place.

As my intellectual reasoning against anxiety became weaker, I found ways to take internal back roads instead of dealing with what had happened inside of me. I found ways to avoid rather than submit to the darkness that lingered around me. In me.

Being busy seemed a reasonably acceptable alternative to dealing with anxiety. Unless sick and forced to, I didn't rest. When I had a moment of downtime from my schedule, I worked at organizing and filling up my schedule to keep everything and everyone going. I had plenty of coffee to keep me fueled up and enough noise from the overflowing calendar to keep those anxious thoughts at bay, so I thought.

The thing with anxiety is this: busyness feeds it.

The schedules, even with our vacations and outings to "rest," often contribute to the whirlwind going on within and around us. When there isn't any space to process life, anxiety takes its grip in an attempt to process for you, but not really. It's more like anxiety takes the driver's seat, and you are tied up in the trunk with duct tape over your mouth.

Simple things become complicated.

When I started to have difficulty with my simple things, like driving, I made time to process the trauma from the past few years. I traded in constantly being on high alert for taking time to go into my room behind closed doors. I stopped *doing* so I could start *feeling*. I concentrated my focus with timed breathing. Memories from the different crises would surface where sometimes I would cry and others where I re-lived the terror from my girls' hospitalizations. I thought

I MADE TIME TO PROCESS THE TRAUMA FROM THE PAST FEW YEARS. I STOPPED *DOING* SO I COULD START *FEELING*.

about the weeks and months leading to my mom's passing. I became thankful for the healing in our tense relationship and thankful she didn't have to hear of her granddaughters' suffering.

Every time I closed the doors, I invited the Holy Spirit to lead me through healing. This took time, over and over again—to breathe, to feel, and to cry. Allowing myself space to remember and feel enlightened me with a healthy perspective instead of being overwhelmed. I let go of the guilt I carried for somehow being responsible for the heartache my family was facing. Then, simple things stopped being complicated.

It felt all better, so I returned to my busy schedule—and kept up that pace for the next several years.

In February 2022, I was recovering from emergency cornea transplant repair surgery. The darkness threatened to disarm me of any strength I had left.

Without my schedule to distract me, I panicked. I felt completely helpless while my rapid heartbeat and shallow breathing offered no options. Prior to my eye crisis, when anxiety would come in closer, I would focus on preparing for whatever was next. I was known to be very organized and punctual in my circles. I had lists for *everything* and volunteered in the activities my kids were involved in. From parent liaison for orchestral groups, field trip coordinator for my sphere of homeschool moms, baseball team mom, and schedules filled with appointments, volunteer opportunities in the community, and scattered dates with my love, I always had something to plan for or think about planning. In more recent years, as my kids grew, I took on more bookkeeping clients and continued to serve in ministry with writing, speaking, and individual prayer and encouragement to those around me.

Breathe in, count, one, two ... out. Again, breathe in a little deeper, one, two, three, four... out. Gasp for air in panic! Try to remember one of the scriptures I memorized for moments like these. Thoughts racing ... *What if? What about ...? Why?* Remember to breathe. *Why isn't this working? What's with the pain in my chest?* Then, I finally did what I should have done hundreds, if not thousands of times before.

With my words barely a whisper, I invited Jesus to come into my darkness.

"Jesus," I murmured, "I know you are there. I'm terrified. I can't feel you. I can't breathe. I can't see," and tears spilled. "Jesus, please come into my darkness with me."

All of my senses changed.

My breathing slowed, and the pain ceased. He was here. I wasn't alone. There was one spot on the couch in which I lay where my family would take turns to sit with me. Jesus came just as my family did and sat with me, bringing me a sense of peace I had never known before. Peace, which calmed all my senses until I fell asleep. When I awoke the next day, I thought maybe it was a dream, but that familiar way that anxiety would linger about me was different. It was like the sky after a big storm—how it looks innocent and promising with hope. The calm brought me the hope I would need for my tomorrows.

When we invite Jesus into the dark areas of our lives—a divorce, the loss of a loved one, a health crisis, fear—name your

SEEING THROUGH THE DARKNESS

darkness—He comes. He comes not as we define Him. He comes as we need Him.

Three of the Gospels recount when Jesus calmed the storm on the sea.[1] Jesus slept through the storm until His disciples awakened Him in fear that they were perishing! "Then He arose and rebuked the winds ... and there was a great calm."[2] Each account indicated Jesus' response to His disciples in regard to their faith: "Why are you so fearful, O you of little faith?"[3] "Why are you so fearful? How is it that you have no faith?"[4] and "Where is your faith?"[5] Jesus calmed the storm and questioned their faith.

Jesus calmed the storm of my anxiety this particular night.

Little did I know, in my ongoing quest against anxiety, I, too, would marvel at the calm Jesus brought to my storm while being left with the question of my faith. Faith I would need to navigate through the terrain ahead. Faith, which the crisis uncovered, had been buried under disappointments. Faith, I tried to fertilize in the soil of my good works. I thought I needed to endure suffering, but somehow, the suffering enabled me to uncover my faith.

THE BEGINNING OF THE END

A good friend shared his testimony about his debilitating battle against anxiety:

I enjoyed my stable life. My wife and I lovingly raised our two boys. I worked in the same career for decades. Until I no longer could. Nothing in my life had changed, yet I endured severe anxiety attacks to the point where I had to be hospitalized multiple times and truly thought I was dying. I gave my sons a farewell charge always to love God even when I passed.

I couldn't work, couldn't eat, couldn't step outside my door to get into my truck.

Then, I met God in a way I had never known before. As a church-attending, Bible-believing Christian of over twenty years, I advise: "If you are dealing with stress and anxiety, take some time to reflect and see where God is. This is where the journey begins."

We limit God with our intellect; as we humble ourselves before the Lord, that's part of the healing process.

The anxiety didn't go away; the journey didn't end with one encounter with God. However, the closeness I grew with the Lord created a springboard for not only my healing, but for my relationships to flourish as I became more vulnerable with loved ones and myself.

I invited Jesus into the mixed-up mental mess where God's voice had become equal to all the other voices vying for my attention.[6]

Anxiety is a common problem. In modern society with myriad pressures, it is an epidemic. In many church circles, mental health still carries a stigma, and sometimes, people are hesitant to admit their struggles for this reason. Be encouraged: there are *many* therapies and tools available for dealing with anxiety. It takes time to discover our individual paths toward healing. My friend and I share our faith in Jesus Christ. I've ridden the roller coaster of lifelong anxiety while his stopped him in his tracks like a freight train. We've both learned the value of making time to mentally and emotionally process life while discovering healthy perspectives. We've relied on loved ones, professionals, and our faith in God.

Unlike my friend, I made the mistake of isolating my anxiety to a series of events. I paused only long enough to grapple with that moment before running back to hiding in my schedule rather than implementing lifestyle changes to sustain me for the long haul. I needed somehow to create the space to process my life while living, but I never took the time to until I was forced to stop again. This time, I was forced to stop with the potential of not only losing my vision, but also possibly losing my eye as well. This time, I had nothing to go back to because everything had changed in a moment. This time, I was forced to figure out how to go forward—somehow—while settling my past.

Despite varying years of counseling, research, and trial and error, I treated my anxiety as my enemy. When I invited Jesus into the moment, I felt the most helpless, yet something changed. Throughout the thirty-plus years of my Christian walk, I invited Him into so many areas of my life. I invited Him into my cluelessness of parenting. I invited Him into the struggles of marriage. I invited Him into navigating my business and our finances. But anxiety had been *my* battle since I was a little girl—and it was a battle I was determined to avoid rather than face. Then, in the darkness with nothing to hide behind, I did what the disciples did in the storm. I called upon Jesus.

He came not only to create calm from the storm but also to bring a reminder of faith.

The darkness and fright of anxiety always lingered nearby; however, Jesus was the light I needed to start looking for my faith.

Change begins when we invite Jesus into our struggles. Our hearts, when left in the darkness, breed dark things. Once we invite Jesus in, we begin to take steps to create space within ourselves where we eventually feel safe enough to start letting others in. This is where the healing begins.

CHANGE BEGINS WHEN WE INVITE JESUS INTO OUR STRUGGLES. OUR HEARTS, WHEN LEFT IN DARKNESS, BREED DARK THINGS.

No longer under the direct assault of the enemy, lying there on the ground, the warrior slept a lot. The pain dissipated. She breathed in deeply during her waking hours, focusing her thoughts on the life she had once known. She remained unaware of how dire her condition had been when she collapsed. The rest—ceasing from the warfare—aided her healing.

She worked hard in everything she did. Too hard. She didn't know when to stop. She would see a need and meet it, especially for those closest to her. She possessed inner strength, which made others feel stronger just by being in her presence. She made others see their value, but she herself lacked faith in her own. Instead, she relied on her accomplishments to gauge her worth. But in her eyes, she could never achieve a worthy status.

Whenever she sensed her own weariness, she'd give herself a quick pep talk to keep going and refused to ask for help or even admit to herself she could use some help.

Shifting movement among those surrounding her interrupted her thoughts. The encirclement about her opened up. Her King stood with His back towards her a short distance ahead.

He looked at her over His shoulder, and He extended His hand. Without a word, she could see the twinkle in His eyes inviting her to join Him.

The same battlefield lay barren before her, but the combat had ceased. She took in the new sense of serenity and saw a large mountain in the direction the King invited her. Fear set in.

She considered the invitation and concluded, *No. Not me. Not now.*

She needed to look at Him, the One who invited her, and not at the invitation itself.

ENDNOTES

1. Matthew 8:23-27, NJKV; Mark 4:35-41, NKJV; and Luke 8:22-25, NKJV.
2. Mark 4:39, NKJV.
3. Matthew 8:26, NKJV.
4. Mark 4:40, NKJV.
5. Luke 8:25, NKJV.
6. Beck, Fred. Testimony on Anxiety shared with Redeeming Love Church. Used with permission.

CHAPTER 3

THE STEWARDSHIP OF SUFFERING

"Your vision will become clear only when you can look into your own heart. Who looks outside, dreams; who looks inside, awakes."

— CARL JUNG
Founder of Analytical Psychology

The warrior kept her eyes fixed on Him. Her vision shifted away from her fears. Away from her past mistakes. Away from the limitations she had been carrying around like Linus from the *Peanuts* cartoon, dragging his beloved blanket everywhere he went. She believed her King could heal the sick, deliver those oppressed from demons, and raise the dead. She knew He could conquer nations, dispel fear, and bring good out of evil.

Her eyes met His, and all thoughts of herself vanished—if only long enough for her to stand and place her hand in His. Nothing else mattered. She forgot everything when she focused on her beloved King.

They walked hand in hand towards the mountain. Her King gave her instructions about some of the terrain ahead. He mentioned something about darkness and a strategy to overcome it. She walked confidently in His presence more than His words, so she didn't listen closely. She remained unaware of anything or anyone other than Him. *Only Him.* Her eyes were fixed on Him as they entered the forest, and darkness surrounded them despite the sun shining high above.

A few weeks after the second cornea transplant, my surgeon caught me off guard, saying, "You've got about 90% of what you are going to have for vision recovery." No, not the second surgery, the second *transplant.* Once I had healed from the initial transplant and the two corresponding surgeries to keep the new cornea in place, my doctors could see a large cataract that took over my lens. Cataract removal would be risky, but necessary.

So, that surgery was scheduled, and I went through another procedure. During the follow-up, my surgeon first exclaimed, "Operating on your eye was like exploring the greatest depths of the ocean with only a flashlight!" Then he explained, "The plan was to remove the cataract and implant a clear lens in its place, but due to the extensive tissue damage, we were unable to implant a lens."

I nodded, "Okay, what does that mean? Can we put a lens in later after my eye has had more time to heal?"

He let out a long, deep sigh, his brow furrowed, and he looked down at his shoes. Adrenalin rushed through me, tasting bitter in my mouth, and my stomach flipped anxiously.

"I'm afraid not," he looked up. "In fact, removing the cataract has damaged the transplanted cornea," he paused, "you will need a new cornea transplant to replace the damaged one, and then I *may* be able to sew a lens in place from the sides since you have lost the integrity to hold a lens in place normally."

My heart sank. "Another transplant?" I whispered, trying to comprehend what that meant. One step forward, five steps back … I sat there, numb. Removing the cataract was supposed to have fixed the problem and allowed me to see again.

It looked like the darkness was going to continue. At least for now. So, we scheduled the second transplant for mid-summer. This surgery was to give me back all the pieces of my eye to determine what I could see again.

My family and I tried to squeeze in some summer fun before the scheduled surgery. It was going to be our last summer as a family of seven. One of the triplets was moving to Florida for grad school. I had planned to drive down with her, but we had to make other arrangements.

My doctors advised me to avoid beaches and sand, so we attempted a staycation of day trips. We started off okay, but our second adventure landed us at emergency services for my youngest son. He looked over his shoulder while taking his last curve on an alpine slide to see if he had beaten his siblings down the popular ski mountain. He simultaneously wiped out and suffered skin burns from the track all over his face, arms, and legs. Each wound had to be cleaned and wrapped independently, and he fractured both ankles. He ended up with casts on both with a set of crutches. End of staycation. In our last family photo before my daughter left, I adorned my eye patch and my youngest his injuries and crutches. I didn't know whether to laugh or cry!

The second transplant went smoother than the first since I no longer had an infection to fight. Because a lens could not be inserted normally, as the procedure usually went for thousands of cataract patients, my surgeon had to sew mine in. During my follow-up appointment, the doctor told me the little bit of light and movement I could recognize out of my right eye was about all the restoration I would have.

I left the office numb.

Once safely in the passenger seat, my tears began to flow. His words landed like a boulder on my chest. The hard, cold, cruel reality that my vision had not recovered—the doctor had said *would not* recover—weighed heavy on me. The nine months of standing in faith and praying for my vision to be restored were behind me. The bitter sting of hopelessness hovered all around. My faith retreated into an abyss of unknowns. The solid ground I had found while contending for a miracle washed away with my tears like a mountain mudslide after a heavy rain.

At this moment, I didn't care *what* the Bible said. I didn't care how my progress had been greater than any of my doctors expected. *I didn't care.* Just let me sit and pet this thing called hopelessness, at least for a little while.

THE INVITATION OF SUFFERING

We send invitations to celebrate and experience cherished moments of our lives with others. To people we know, to people we love, and to people we trust. We extend invitations to those whom we want to look back and remember the significance of a shared moment. Suffering, on the other hand, comes in like an unwelcome house guest with no indication of how long the stay will be.

The invitation of suffering comes to me and you, my fellow sojourner, with the request to embark upon a journey to find strength we didn't know we could possess, relationships we didn't know we needed, and to create movement in our lives that we may not have otherwise known.

We can *ignore* the invitation and stay right where our defining moment stopped us in our tracks. Here, our emotions prevail and preside. Anger, bitterness, and cynicism set in, and instead of us using them to progress through the circumstance, they stay the course and resist every opportunity for change.

Alternatively, we can *acknowledge* the invitation. In doing this, we accept our new circumstances as our lot in life. We are no longer consumed with the raw, negative feelings, and we make peace with what has happened. The sense of peace brings a false sense of contentment, where we settle with the current outcome, but we remain unable or unwilling to contend with our faith.

Or, we can *accept* the invitation—an invitation to navigate new terrain with our faith, where we process the emotions, press beyond contentment, and become willing to be vulnerable in uncertainty. Here, we may wrestle with questioning God. Here, we step out into the darkness of the unknown to adjust our vision and experience life in ways we never have before.

WILL YOU ACCEPT THE INVITATION TO STEP OUT INTO THE DARKNESS OF THE UNKNOWN?

Some days, I tried to ignore the invitation, hoping if I didn't pay attention to what had happened to me, then it would all just go away. Once I was feeling a little better and able to get off the couch, my normal tasks were quick reminders of my new ailment. I struggled with depth perception in areas I once took for granted. I couldn't tell when my pen would touch the paper on the table. I couldn't see when someone or something approached me on my right side. I couldn't tell when my feet would find uneven trails once I returned to hiking, so I would stomp, overstep, baby step, and try to feel my way with my poles through rocky terrain.

When I actually acknowledged my invitation, I began to make peace with the loss of vision and figure out my "new normal." I purposed to accept my limitations and discover new ways to deal with challenges. For example, I felt sad at first when I couldn't drive, and my four older kids took turns taking me to my appointments. But I adjusted to being chauffeured around; I passed the time on my phone in the passenger seat and complained about the music and temperature in the car. Talk about coming full circle!

But I also became frustrated. Frustrated by my new limitations and how different my life had become. Acknowledging the changes left me feeling defeated. I questioned if living a life of faith had to be more than a cycle of praying and either getting answers to prayer or learning to live with the disappointment of unanswered prayers. My faith wobbled. The bedrock of my beliefs rumbled like a far-off earthquake had sent aftershocks beneath my once-solid ground. I was angry. I was angry at myself for being angry.

When suffering knocked on my door, I wanted to run out the back door and find a new residence. But this invitation implored me to change in ways I otherwise could not.

So, I accepted my invitation, and a journey opened up before me. A journey of rocky, treacherous unknowns. When getting back to normal left me restless, I began to recognize I needed to become more vulnerable with the one person I spent the most time with—myself. This required courage to wrestle with mindsets and behavior patterns I had spent a lifetime trying to either ignore or deny. It was a new terrain I felt desperately ill-equipped to navigate, but I needed to discover it all at the same time.

Once I accepted the invitation to suffering, I wrestled with *Why would God let me suffer?*

I had to look beyond myself, where religious mindsets caused me to question if I had done something wrong, which now caused me to suffer. *God is good. God is my Father. Provider. Protector. If something this bad has happened to me, then I must have done something bad to deserve it, right? Or else, God is not good ... no! I can't reconcile that. God is good. But if God is good, then why would He let me suffer?* The cycle of internal dialogue was torture.

When I pressed into these thoughts, over time, I discovered the nature of God. His *kindness* became more real to me. The Holy Spirit manifested the presence of God, and He sat with me—reminded me He was there. He didn't promise me what the outcome would look like, or what I would like; He just promised He would be there with me. A beautiful promise I had been aiming and striving for all my life. I just wanted to know He was there; I just wanted to know I was good enough. In the suffering, I experienced how there wasn't anything I could do to make Him love me. He loves me because of who He is.

GETTING TO THE OTHER SIDE

We don't have to stay in neutral when a crisis hits. Suffering has another side. We may not be able to move toward it yet or have any idea in which direction to start, but there is another side. I didn't know how to get there. I just knew I couldn't get to the other side by sitting around. I needed some kind of movement.

Dr. Geoff Warburton shares in his *TED Talk,* "The Adventure of Grief," how twenty-five years of research taught him the same lessons he learned about grief from watching his two grandmothers mourn their separate losses. One survived, and one thrived. One avoided the process of moving through grief; the other saw the depth of the pain, loss, and chasm of dark emotions as a passage. According to his memories of his grandmothers, one said, "Why me?" and the other, "Why not me?"[1]

Once medically cleared, I spent a lot of time hiking. I struggled to see the terrain while adjusting to both lost vision in one eye and wearing glasses, neither of which I was accustomed to. I posted on social media after most of my hikes, sharing what I relearned and the struggles I encountered. I wanted to remember. Sharing my experience helped me assign it meaning. It was therapeutic. I had to restart my endurance level and determine realistic elevation gains based on my limitations. Things I once took for granted brought new experiences as I sorted through how tree cover, sunlight, and shadows affected my vision.

I hated what I saw in the mirror. My eye was not only misshapen, but it also lacked an iris—the beautiful color surrounding the eye's pupil. My husband had been calling me *Green Eyes* since we were dating over twenty-five years ago, and I have been "Green Eyes" as a contact in his phone. Even with the other scars on my body, I'd never felt loss so intense or personal. My eye looked grotesque to me. It had an irregular hole in the middle of the white sclera, and it looked like a prop from a horror or sci-fi film.

It wasn't feminine or pretty. If it was a "window to my soul," then my soul had gone rogue.

At times, I would sit and wallow. Once, in a particular moment, I looked in the mirror, and my surgical eye looked bloodshot and wounded as if I had just been in a fight. I realized my emotional state over what had taken place was, in a sense, beating myself up.

I avoided people as I tried to make peace with what happened. Hiking during the peak of fall foliage while taking in the brilliance of the colors transformed my perspective. I noticed my mood became lighter. I experienced different trails, taking in views with my one eye—enormously grateful for that eye and counting the blessing of even one-eyed vision—while feeling the profound loss of vision in my other eye, the damage of perspective, and the hindrance of my visual field. Gratitude and grief intermingled, and at the same time, I experienced an unexpected awakening. I didn't know it until I found it, but I kept looking for beauty in nature. Watching the dramatic changes to the landscape as the vibrance of autumn quickly faded to bare trees as winter approached reminded me of the amazing beauty to behold in nature—and the beauty helped me to take another step forward.

CREATE YOUR MOVEMENT

Warburton also shared how his thriving grandmother would bake, sew, and perform a variety of other homemaking activities to create movement in her life. One of my triplets started playing violin at eight years old. We learned together how she uniquely processes life. She doesn't care for journaling, hiking, or even talking much, all of which are tools I use to process life. She'd rather engulf herself in music, playing, listening, and now composing as her therapy.

She had to re-evaluate her future as a music performance major in college and adjust to the changes COVID forced upon the world with the possibility of not having career options. During this time, her college also announced their plan to close the music school at the end of her graduating class.

Her college experience became a heavy heartache on her soul. She not only had to navigate through the turmoil the worldwide virus placed upon our young people, but she also felt the pain of a long-time, well-known music school closing its doors. She'd been working with several of the professors and music instructors for years prior to even becoming their student. They were now friends and had been teaching at the music school for decades, and she witnessed them losing their jobs.

I watched her battle the confusion and anger, along with hopelessness and concern for her peers and professors.

One year later, we were thankful to sit in person for her senior violin recital and the final orchestra performance of the music school. Nostalgia stirred in my heart as I sat in the beautiful auditorium in which I had been attending concerts for years.

My daughter stepped on stage, commanding her instrument and not only the audience's attention, but also their utmost respect. She memorized all her music, including the well-known Bach's *Chaconne*, and she played flawlessly. Then, she closed out her recital with pieces she had composed.

The orchestra completed their season playing her original composition, *Out of the Darkness*. She shared in the program and before the attendees how she wrote this piece to process all of the darkness she was witnessing around her, from the COVID shutdowns to now the music school closing.

Right there in that moment, all who had the privilege of being in attendance witnessed how Rachael made it through to the other side. She, through her composing and playing, not only found her way to the other side, but brought others along with her.

A beloved colleague in the local music community who had been walking through tremendous grief shared, through tears after the performance, how hearing this piece brought her through her darkness.

We were created for movement.

It's in the movement where we make our way to the other side. Your mountain may have a higher elevation than mine, or even a longer distance. May I remind you, my fellow sojourner, to create your movement. Maybe it's in knitting or baking. Maybe it's in sending a handwritten card to someone suffering or trying that physical challenge you have been thinking about for years. There are countless opportunities if we are willing to look.

OFFER COMFORT

Whispers, side glances, and some obvious finger-pointing. One way or another, we experience the separation between the one who suffers and those around them. As onlookers, we measure what others go through based on what we ourselves think we can endure. There seems to be superhero-like strength available to those suffering, which we can't come up with on our own.

> AS ONLOOKERS, WE MEASURE WHAT OTHERS GO THROUGH BASED ON WHAT WE OURSELVES THINK WE CAN ENDURE.

It's completely natural to step back from those who are suffering. We don't want to burden them and add more to their already overflowing plate, which is good and necessary. But what if our suffering loved one doesn't need us to fix the pain or even try to make it go away?

What if they just need you by their side? The ministry of presence. The beauty of comfort with no attempt to answer, resolve, or explain the suffering at all.

Jesus experienced this when He brought three of the disciples near as He went to pray in the garden just before His arrest. He knew His friends couldn't take the cup from Him or for Him. Yet, His humanity longed for the comfort of those closest to Him to be nearby in prayer during His great distress.

SEEING THROUGH THE DARKNESS

I received a gift of colorful eyepatches from a friend. I had fun choosing which eye patch would coordinate best with my outfits. I really liked the cheetah print eyepatch to go with my cheetah print blouse. I appreciated the gift I never would have bought for myself.

This colorful bag of eyepatches carried a message I didn't know I needed. It didn't stir my faith, it didn't remind me of what my life used to be, or cast any vision—no pun intended—for my tomorrow. This colorful bag of eye patches showed me I was okay even if I *wasn't* okay.

The gift helped me acknowledge my condition and brought me strength and courage to take another step on my journey.

It's such a delicate dance to let others know we care when they suffer. We wonder if our words of encouragement help. I promise you, they do. Keep sending the texts even if you don't get a response right away, offer to make another meal, and find beauty in being willing just to come and sit with them. If you aren't part of their inner circle, let me encourage you to still reach out. You may be the very support the person needs.

When we are hurting, we long for a sense of normal, a normal we know is gone, but crave nonetheless. Meet your suffering loved ones in the middle of their pain. Be the normal they have lost.

STEPPING OUT

With my family, eyepatch matching my outfit, and my nails freshly done, I attended a gathering to celebrate a loved one's recent accomplishments. A few hours later, I staggered to the car overcome with emotion. Through hot tears, I questioned why I had to be treated differently, sorted through shallow comments, and wondered if more than just my appearance changed. Had I missed something others could see?

I no longer viewed life the same way. Affliction changed me. Enduring the trials I walked through and the choices I made in the midst of my suffering framed—re-framed—my tomorrows. Suffering summoned me from one place to another.

Accepting my invitation to suffering led me through sorrow. A season I would rather have skipped, but I am thankful to have endured. In the places where I created space to grieve and mourn what I lost, I discovered beauty and goodness again.

Our vision changes when we suffer. We see life through a different lens, even when our suffering has nothing to do with our eyes. Suffering enables us to look at ourselves more honestly, admit our faults, see our strengths, and become vulnerable to admit we don't have all the answers. Our vision adjusts to where we see how our life isn't really about what has happened to us, but how we choose to respond.

Maybe your body became altered from medical treatments, or maybe you feel like used goods from relationships gone bad. Maybe your identity took a hit from a financial loss or a forced career change. In every loss, there always remains beauty to discover and movement to create. Whatever our suffering is, it has been trusted to us. Trusted to bring the pain of disappointments, heartache of unwelcome change, and longing for hope in our tomorrows to God, in faith.

Use your courage to accept the invitation of suffering. Remember that doing so doesn't mean you just surrender to the unpleasantness of your circumstances, but you create your own movement. Give yourself permission to mourn what you once had and even what could have or should been but isn't. And on the really hard days, I pray you find the kindness you long for from others inside yourself.

Suffering isn't a destination; it is a journey to bring us from where we once were to another place. A place where life will never be how it once was, but it still can be beautiful.

The trail narrowed, so the warrior walked closely behind the King. She breathed in the fresh, crisp air of pines, mixing with the variety of greenery that littered the forest floor. Within minutes, her heart rate began to climb with her steps. The dense tree cover opened up to reveal a steep upward ascent of rocks of all shapes and sizes as far as the eyes could see. She had to keep her focus on her footing, so she lost sight of the King.

As her breathing became more labored, the warrior's thoughts also became more erratic. *Am I really physically able to be doing this right now?* Her pace slowed; she still couldn't see the King. *Did He consider my abilities before bringing me out here?* The unpredictable terrain shift took her off guard. Steep inclines with rock scrambles replaced the serenity she had enjoyed at the lower elevation. Both her thoughts and physical abilities negotiated through the challenges of the terrain. She grasped at exposed tree roots to climb her way through the steep, rocky elevation gain. *What if I can't make it? What if I lose my grip?*

Why can't I see my King? What if I get lost?

With contentment long since faded, the familiar banter of lies flooded her mind and soul.

ENDNOTE

1. Warburton, Geoff, Dr. TEDxBrighton, "The Adventure of Grief." Accessed from https://www.youtube.com/watch?v=juET61B1P98 on February 22, 2021.

C H A P T E R 4

THE SUPERPOWER OF GRACE

"For by grace you have been saved through faith,
and that not of yourselves; it is the gift of God,
not of works, lest anyone should boast."
— E P H E S I A N S   2 : 8 - 9 ,   N K J V

I am thankful for my Roman-Catholic upbringing. Every Sunday, my mom made sure she and I were in church. Some of my greatest memories were celebrating Easter, year after year, cramming into an overflowing church with a new dress, bonnet, and patent leather shoes.

I appreciated learning about Jesus Christ. I would sometimes stare at the statue high above the altar depicting the crucified

Jesus. I often wondered why one man endured so much torture to forgive the sins of all mankind. As a young adult, I became more curious to understand God.

While in college, recovering from a jet ski accident, I was mindlessly clicking through T.V. stations and stopped when a minister spoke words that seemed aimed directly at me. I joined him in prayer as we called upon the Lord Jesus Christ. I repented for my sins, accepted Jesus' payment for my sins through His death and resurrection, and welcomed Him as my Savior and Lord. By faith, I chose to receive the remarkable gift of grace of eternal salvation. As I prayed, I noticed a great weight lifted off my heavy soul. And I had no understanding of what had happened.

I lost a semester of college while I recovered from the surgery where a permanent metal plate was inserted from my knee to my ankle. With a cast from my ankle to my hip, I didn't leave the house very much, yet there was an awakening happening inside me. Something seemed different when I tried to return to my former lifestyle of partying. Once back on my feet, I embarked on finding a church with my newfound zeal to learn more about God. I eventually settled into a non-denominational church. However, I quickly discovered that my faith rose and fell like waves in the ocean. I had hoped Christianity would keep me from pain and hardship. Instead, I had to learn how to use my faith in the middle of the pain and challenges life brings.

So, I worked at my faith. I engulfed my life in "good works." I volunteered in multiple ways at church and in the community. I attended meetings and conferences to grow in my knowledge of Christian customs and teachings. As days turned into years, I hosted Bible studies and prayer groups while continuing to serve at church and in the community.

I expected God to respond to my demands for provision, healing, or anything else I deemed necessary to bring comfort into my life so I wouldn't have to endure discomfort for very long. I wanted to call the shots, and when I said I had had enough, He needed to come through for me. My faith was operating at the highest levels right there. All the while, unknowingly, I attempted to use my good works and good deeds to earn good graces with God.

When I faced the threat of losing my eye, I quoted scriptures on healing in an attempt to dictate *how* God should heal me, *when* He should heal me, and *why* He should heal me. In all actuality, I had been standing on my doctrine of good deeds. I felt like God owed me because of the things I did for Him, as an expression of my faith, of course.

While recovering from the third surgery on my eye, I lamented the outcome. When the cataract removal not only failed to recover my vision but damaged the first cornea transplant, I kept trying to figure out what went wrong. The results of the surgery didn't remotely come close to what I had been praying for. I didn't want to be mad at God. But I was.

In the parable of the Prodigal Son, we read the story of a father with two sons.[1] The reckless son persuaded his father to give him his inheritance. He left home and squandered his inheritance on wild living. He ended up caring for pigs with nowhere to go. One day, he determined his father should at least take him back as a servant, as the hired help. And his father cared for his hired help well. So, he headed home.

His father longed for the day his son would return and saw him coming from afar. The father didn't care how his son smelled from having been with the pigs, nor that he returned with nothing to show for his inheritance—he had returned home. The father embraced his son and called his servants to bring the best robe, a ring, and sandals for his feet—without even telling him to shower first! This is how God feels about us. He doesn't care about the state in which we come; He just wants us to come because He is the Father who longs for us.

When the elder brother returned from the field and learned the reason for the party, he did not react well.

"The older brother became angry and refused to go in. So his father went out and pleaded with him. But he answered his father, 'Look! All these years I've been slaving for you and never disobeyed your orders. Yet you never gave me even a young goat so I could celebrate with my friends. But when this son of yours who has squandered your property with prostitutes comes home, you kill the fattened calf for him!'

"'My son,' the father said, 'you are always with me, and everything I have is yours. But we had to celebrate and be glad, because this brother of yours was dead and is alive again; he was lost and is found.'"[2]

The older brother didn't care about the grace his father extended to his younger brother because he thought he didn't need it himself. The older brother only pointed out his good deeds to his father, completely unaware that the same grace in his father's heart towards his prodigal brother was also available to him. The older brother could not see his father's character. He was too busy trying to judge his father through the eyes of his deeds. When we make our works about ourselves, our status, or our good standing with God, we miss out on the grace that is available to us daily.

IS GRACE GOD'S "UNMERITED" OR "UNDESERVED" FAVOR?"

The gift of grace, an undeserved gift, is one which we often don't understand. Scripture offers over one hundred uses of the term *grace*, mostly in the New Testament, and the Apostle Paul addressed the subject of grace more than any other author in his writings to the church. Through grace, God provided a means for us to spend eternity with Him. Yet, grace offers us even more than the wonderful gift of salvation. God gives us grace as a superpower for our daily living and the challenges we face— *especially* when we suffer.

We Christians often adorn our lives with works. Yours may look like some combination of church attendance, daily devotional time, giving to the poor, and taking mission trips. It may include attending a small group, volunteering at a food pantry, or helping out an aging neighbor. All of these things are great—essential

SEEING THROUGH THE DARKNESS

> IF WE ARE FILLING OUR LIVES UP WITH WORKS IN AN EFFORT TO GAIN A BETTER STANDING WITH GOD, WE ARE MISSING GRACE.

for Christian living. However, if we are filling our lives up with works in an effort to gain a better standing with God, we are missing grace. Regardless of what our works are or how many works we do, they will *never* earn us grace. Grace is a free gift from God available to those who believe in Jesus Christ. When we ask Jesus to be the Lord of our lives, it doesn't mean we've been hired to do works for Him, either. Rather, Jesus welcomes us into His family with all the perks of being a family member, one in particular being grace.

We will end up frustrated time and time again, like the elder brother to the prodigal son, when we make our Christian lives about fulfilling religious duties. Trust me, I've tried. It keeps you busy checking off good behavior boxes, but it doesn't leave you fulfilled. We can never complete enough works to earn God's grace and God will not go against His own word to extend us grace for our works.

Paul wrote, "Now to the one who works, wages are not credited as a gift but as an obligation. However, to the one who does not work but trusts God who justifies the ungodly, their faith is credited as righteousness."[3]

Friends, to receive grace, we must cease from the works we've been doing to try to earn it. Instead, we must trust God to *receive* grace—like we receive our salvation—as a free gift. To do so, we must humble ourselves. It's a lot easier to put in effort toward receiving something so we can take some credit for the outcome.

When my triplets plus one were little, I needed grace around the clock. My cluelessness created a desperation to rely on God. When my triplets were infants, I somehow managed their three-hour feedings, pumping milk in between, the clean-up, diaper changes, and laundry with grace ... *and* my spreadsheet to keep track of everything! It was a lot of work, but I used my faith to access grace in my daily life.

Paul also wrote, "But He said to me, 'My grace is sufficient for you, for My power is made perfect in weakness. Therefore I will boast all the more gladly about my weakness,' so that Christ's power may rest on me."[4]

We need grace for daily living. Let's not get caught up thinking that we *only* need grace for the hard things or to run ministries. We need grace. Every. Single. Day. For our families, our jobs, businesses, and relationships.

"And God *is* able to make all grace abound toward you, that you, always having all sufficiency in *all* things, may have an abundance for every good work."[5]

God provides us with the grace to do things we otherwise could not do on our own.

When I made my faith about my deeds, I got off the trail, so to speak. I couldn't exercise my faith as I needed to. When life didn't go the way I demanded in prayer, I became angry. I lost sight of grace. I felt like I had earned it, so I felt cheated when it didn't manifest in the way I defined it. We use our faith to *receive* grace. We can't earn it. I had it backward. I cannot earn grace—I can only receive it—and only then by faith.

Grace not only enables us to navigate through our daily lives better, but also empowers us to do amazing things for God. Grace enables us to enjoy our works as an expression of thanksgiving to God rather than checking off the items on our religious duties list. Here, where our works meet with God's grace, we accomplish things we never thought we could. Our prayer lives and Bible reading find new momentum. Church and small groups become more exciting, and acts of service, more fulfilling.

SAVED *FOR* GOOD WORKS— NOT *BY* GOOD WORKS

Deborah, the prophetess, held a position as a judge in Israel. The people of Israel had been under the oppression of King Jabin of Canaan for twenty years, and the Lord responded when the people cried out to Him for help from the oppression. Deborah summoned Barak, the military commander. Under the prophetic instruction of Deborah, Barak accepted the invitation to lead God's people to victory as long as Deborah would go with him. But Deborah warned Barak that if she went with him, he would not

THE SUPERPOWER OF GRACE

receive any glory in the victory, for the Lord would deliver Sisera, the commander of Jabin's army, into the hands of a woman.

Furthermore, Deborah instructed Barak on when to engage in battle. The entire enemy army fell to God's people, except for Sisera, the enemy commander, who fled to the tent of Jael, wife of Heber the Kenite. Heber's alliance caused him to be at peace with the enemy of God's people, so Sisera assumed he would be safe in Heber's home. He did not take into account Heber's wife, Jael, a God-fearing woman. She welcomed Sisera as a guest with a blanket and some milk. Sisera, cozy and warm, fell fast asleep.

With his guard down as he slept, Jael took a tent peg and a hammer and drove the spike into his temple.[6]

Talk about a warrior!

This story carries many messages, but I want to talk about how God used two different women. One was a working woman, Deborah, and the other was Jael, a homemaker, or should we say tent maker. Neither woman let anyone get in her way of not only believing God, the God of Israel, but also in doing whatever He put in their hearts. Deborah served as a judge at a time when women were not seen in these types of positions, and she spoke prophetically during a desperate time in Israel. Jael didn't let her husband's allegiance to the enemy stand in the way of what she needed to do to avenge the way of the Lord.

Two women serving the same God. Two women who used their faith and the works they had been given to serve the Lord. They didn't use their actions in an effort to gain God's favor; they used their faith to guide their actions.

If they had taken the approach to use their positions in an attempt to avenge God's people in their own timing or their own strength, the outcome could have been disastrous and possibly cost them their own lives. When we align our works with God, His purposes prevail, even when they are a little bloody.

When we base our good works on us, we often find frustration. The very things we have committed to do as good works to fill us instead become the very things that leave us empty.

Should we quit trying and go back to the ways we once lived? No! We need to adjust our *intent*. I wore myself out with my good works as I tried to prove my worth to an audience of One. Unbeknown to me, I had been the only one keeping track of my seemingly good deeds—God was not impressed.

Our works need to be an overflow of our expression of thanksgiving, not our means to reach God. When we make our works about our attempt to reach God, we lose sight of our faith, which can create the potential to develop a narcissistic platform with no room for God. Our works become our idols, and we step out of His sufficiency to become self-sufficient even while willing to give God credit for "the assist" when things go well. God created us for good works as an extension of Himself in the earth, not for us to draw attention to ourselves.

God designed us to live fulfilled lives where He not only equips us for our calling, but has unique purposes designed for us. We will never be fulfilled until we discover who He has created us to be. Only then can we turn our attention to what He has for us to do. His grace enables us to make things come into being. God's grace makes the impossible possible. Grace is a:

G – Gift from God

R – Received by faith

A – Available every day

C – Ceased from trying to earn by works

E – Encountered in every situation

She kept climbing the long, rocky trail. Her lungs burned. Her head throbbed. The rocks blurred before her when she tried to look ahead. She felt desperately alone as she tried to steady her thoughts between deciding which rocks were friends or foes.

Why do I need to climb this stupid mountain anyway? I'm not really up to it, nor am I enjoying it. It's hard. I'm hot ... Irritable and irrational, she could hardly stand her own company.

Off in the distance, she heard the sound of moving water. It was inviting, which caused her to push on. Her legs shook from the climb when the terrain leveled out. She reached the waters to discover small falls cascading into pools of refreshing water. She sat on a large rock to pause and catch her breath, observing the ebb and flow of water swirling over different-sized rocks. She welcomed the rest as she focused on the mini waterfalls forming alongside smaller pools of water in a delicate dance.

She longed for her life to be as graceful as the water she watched. It seemed carefree, while her life seemed more like a series of constant, treacherous upward rock climbs like the one she had just endured.

The voice of the King rose gently above the water, "I am so happy you accepted My invitation!"

He came alongside her as He spoke. "I want to remind you of a couple of things to focus on when you feel like you want to give up. Remember, I love you, and there isn't anything you can do to make Me love you any more or any less. I love you because I am Love. Pay attention to challenges when you feel overwhelmed. You have fought with the same issues over and over again, and they are familiar to you. Now, you will see them for what they really are and discover how to overcome them. When you focus on My love for you, you will find strength."

She wanted to answer Him, but she didn't know what to say. All her words of complaint melted like wax in His presence. His nearness filled her with peace, replacing all thoughts of how unfair things were or wondering why she had to endure such hard things.

In His light, all her shadows faded.

The King continued, "There will be more times when you may not see Me. When this happens, you have a choice to make. When the darkness in your mind overwhelms you, you must choose what you believe. You can believe lies about Me and lies about yourself, but these will keep you living in defeat. Or you can believe the truth—the truth you know—and it will set you free."[7]

Her eyes met His. She was lost in His gaze. Secure. Resolute.

She heard rustling in the woods and her eyes searched the horizon; a familiar panic rose inside her, and she felt small again. And afraid.

"Will you believe the truth regardless of how things look?" the King asked.

With tears streaming down her face, she whispered, "How? I don't know how."

"You have been given a measure of faith, dear warrior," He lifted her chin to meet His gaze, "faith you must use to believe in Me. But now you must also use your faith to remember who I say you are."

She nodded, feeling hope she could not explain.

"As you endure challenges here," He continued, "you will discover strength you didn't know you possessed—*especially* when you can't see Me. Your faith connects you to Me and will enable you to endure the challenges you face.

"Use your faith to remind yourself who you are and dispel lies when they try to paralyze you and hold you back. Remember, my sweet one, I have chosen you for this journey ... not to break you or destroy you—but to show you *Who. You. Are.* To teach you to trust *Me.* You defeat yourself when you believe lies. Lies about what you can do and who you are. You don't need to understand the terrain; you need only to trust Me."

She weighed His words. They kindled embers deep in her heart, coaxing them into flame. She did use her faith to believe in Him; that was the easy part. But to use her faith regarding herself—that seemed like a stretch—even when He was near.

He smiled, "Just remember, this journey isn't about the physical terrain. You are on a path toward freedom against the captivity of your own mind. Stand upon the truth of who I say you are, and you will find victory against the darkness."

ENDNOTES

1. See Luke 15:11-32.
2. Luke 15:28-32, NIV.
3. Romans 4:4-5, NIV.
4. 2 Corinthians 12:9, NIV.
5. 2 Corinthians 9:8, NKJV.
6. Read Judges 4 for the full account of Deborah and Jael.
7. See John 8:32.

CHAPTER 5

CHANGED BY GRACE

*"No one ever injured their eyesight
looking on the bright side of things."*
— ANONYMOUS

In *The Chronicles of Narnia: The Voyage of the Dawn Treader,* beloved little Lucy has grown into a beautiful young lady. But Lucy doesn't see her own beauty; she longs to look like her older sister, Susan, who never lacked admirers.

While on her journey with Prince Caspian and crew to recover the lost swords of Narnia, Lucy discovers a book of incantations. In her search to undo a spell upon the land surrounding her, she finds a spell to claim greater beauty. As her quest for beauty always lingers, Lucy quickly rips the page out of the book to use in privacy. She waits until just the right moment, hidden away in her room, where she utters the "Beauty Enchantment." Within moments of doing so, she walks into a vision alongside her brothers at a party. She enjoys the attentiveness of those admiring her beauty like she had witnessed many times with her sister Susan. Reality awakens her when a sibling photo was taken for her parents—a photo of her two brothers and the image of Susan. When Lucy (as Susan) inquires about Lucy's whereabouts, she panics when she realizes she has almost wished herself away. She awakens to see the lion, Aslan (C.S. Lewis' depiction of Christ).

Aslan explains to Lucy how she chose her sister's beauty over her own, and in doing so, she practically wished herself away. He continued, pointing out to her how none of her siblings would have discovered Narnia had it not been for Lucy.

Right before walking away, Aslan gives Lucy a reminder we all need: "You doubt your value. Don't run from who you are."

Lucy couldn't see her own beauty.

Lucy was unaware of her value.

What is missing in our lives because of the lies we believe?

IS THIS MY THOUGHT?

Various studies indicate an individual averages 50,000-70,000 thoughts per day, with 70-80% being negative. If we break the percentages down, we can have 40,000 negative thoughts a day![1] We need to become aware of our thoughts so that we can gain control over them. What we think about becomes evident in how we live and the choices we make. Just because a thought passes through our minds doesn't mean we have to accept it as our own.

For years, I allowed my thoughts to take up real estate in my mind as my own. Thoughts about how I lacked worth, thoughts about how my relationships were unsatisfying, thoughts about how I couldn't achieve my goals—and I lived as such.

Any life coach, weight loss coach, or self-help guru will tell us how our thoughts have power over our lives. Coaches teach and guide us where to focus our thoughts. We need a standard to guide and filter our thoughts so we can choose what we allow to remain and entertain as part of what we process and contemplate.

Many people base their standards on their goals. Suppose we work toward being a competitive weightlifter and have thoughts of eating donuts and ice cream invading our minds. In that case, we recognize these thoughts as destructive to our goal and choose to ignore them, or at least put them aside, until after the competition.

While it may not have too much of an effect if we were to give into eating donuts and ice cream once, we can kiss good competition results goodbye if we succumb to those thoughts over and over again.

When we choose the Word of God as our standard, we have a sure measurement for our thoughts to determine truth vs. a lie.

We can use the Bible to recognize the enemy's lies and combat them with the truth in the scriptures.

As we align our thoughts with God's, we find grace and strength to navigate through life's circumstances and discover our value among many other great treasures. When our thoughts or even the words of others tell us something contrary, you and I can choose not to listen to them, just like the weightlifter doesn't have to give into the thoughts of donuts and ice cream.

> BELIEVING LIES KEEPS US NOT ONLY FROM OUR GOALS BUT ALSO FROM ACCESSING THE GRACE GOD HAS FOR US.

Believing lies keeps us not only from our goals but also from accessing the grace God has for us. Once we pay attention to what we are thinking about, we can access the grace that empowers us to stop cycles of defeat and dysfunction.

I had a choice to accept or reject what I saw when I looked in the mirror. The experience of seeing how my negative thoughts toward my eye caused it to look wounded one day in the mirror sobered me. I didn't want to treat myself harshly anymore. I had a real-time visual illustration of what my negative self-talk was doing. I decided instead to confront the negative thoughts toward my appearance with the truth. I started by looking at myself in the mirror. I looked at the eye that could no longer look back at me, and I told myself I was loved. I would tell myself the reminder I needed for the moment: *God loves me. My husband loves me. I love me.*

Making peace with my situation like this felt raw and, at times, emotional. I couldn't say much more when I initially started because of how hard I would cry. Saying the words was not an instant victory. Saying the words was a battle. It was striking blows against the lies I believed. Over time and with consistency, I worked up to speaking scriptures on healing over myself out loud. No one else could come and provide the courage God's grace gave me to step outside what my feelings and thoughts were trying to dictate and bring me the truth I needed to frame my future.

What do you need God's grace to accept, friend? Maybe your body changed dramatically from cancer treatments, or an accident left you permanently marred. Maybe you struggle with feeling like used goods after your marriage fell apart. Whatever it is—your skin color, your hair, the shape of your body ... Instead of cringing every time you look in the mirror, start repeating words of life, love, and affirmation over yourself. When God looks at you, He smiles. Let's learn to smile back. God will fill us with His grace when we apply the truth of His Word to our lives.

———————

In Genesis, Eve questioned God and listened to the enemy whisper his lies to her. She accepted these lies as her truth and acted upon what she believed with disastrous consequences. Like Eve, we become susceptible to the lies of the enemy when we don't believe God. When we establish lies instead of truth, we lose our sense of self. We often find ourselves longing for someone else's marriage, job, or house. We'll desire someone else's body or relationships. The lies become so prevalent that, like Lucy in Narnia, we practically wish our lives away.

SPEAK YOUR TRUTH

We live in a time where you have your truth, and I have mine. Sometimes, we agree, and other times, we don't. Our opinions matter to Oprah, social media, and the enemy of our souls. Our enemy loves to hear us say, "I think," "I feel," and even "I believe."

As believers, our beliefs don't really matter. I am serious. What I believe as a believer doesn't matter unless what I believe lines up with the truth. The truth is found in the Word of God—the Bible. It is the only source of truth trustworthy enough to serve as our standard of measure.

To fully access grace, we must know the truths of God's Word. "For the law was given through Moses; but grace and truth came through Jesus Christ."[2] Grace and truth are given to us through Jesus.

I don't know about you, but I can't rely on my feelings and desires to dictate my truth. Feelings are as unpredictable as the weather, and desires rotate like a carousel at the fair. What great victory the enemy gains when we agree with our own opinions more than the standard given to us from the Word of God.

We will always have chaos when we choose to live by our own standards. We need a higher standard—truth—to thrive.

Not too long ago, I called to make a hotel reservation. The young man who answered my call kept saying, "I *believe* there is an availability for those dates." He continued, "I *feel* there is availability for those dates." Honestly, I didn't care what he believed or how he felt; I just needed the truth of whether or not they actually had availability for those dates.

We cannot govern our lives by our feelings or beliefs if we don't have something concrete to stand upon. The truth we believe and profess becomes the foundation upon which we base our lives. When the foundation we choose changes with trends, culture, and what others say about us, we subject ourselves to heartache and uncertainty.

> THE TRUTH WE BELIEVE AND PROFESS BECOMES THE FOUNDATION UPON WHICH WE BASE OUR LIVES.

When we recognize the Bible as our measurement of truth, we have a standard to determine the thoughts we want to entertain. Paul instructs us to cast down arguments (philosophies and cultural norms) and every high thing (opinions or priorities) that exalts themselves above God. He tells us to bring our thoughts into captivity to the obedience of Christ.[3] In his letter to the Philippians, Paul sums it up like this: "Finally, brothers and sisters, whatever is true, whatever is noble, whatever is right, whatever is pure, whatever is lovely, whatever is admirable—if anything is excellent or praiseworthy—think about such things."[4]

Look at the very first thing in the list Paul gave us to direct our thoughts toward—*truth*! When we read over the remaining items on the list, not one of them leaves room for thinking negatively about anyone or anything, including ourselves.

God Himself sets the example for us to follow because, ultimately, God thinks good thoughts toward you and me. "'For I know the thoughts that I think toward you,' says the LORD, 'thoughts of peace and not of evil, to give you a future and a hope.'"[5] My friend, you are constantly in God's thoughts—how incredible!

"Every single moment, You are thinking of me! How precious and wonderful to consider that You cherish me constantly in Your every thought! O God, Your desires toward me are more than the grains of sand on every shore! When I awake in the morning, you're still with me."[6]

God sees you and is thinking lovingly about you. He cherishes you and delights in you.

In this thought, my heart finds comfort: We don't have to accept negative thoughts as our own, and we have a standard of truth to measure our thoughts toward.

THE ATTITUDE OF JOB

You are likely familiar with the story of Job in the Bible. Job lived a blessed life. He had a wife, a large family, land, animals, and servants to help take care of it all. Then, one day, a conversation took place between God and Satan. God pointed to Job for Satan to consider. The same God who blessed Job and placed the hedge of protection upon him sent a referral to Satan to test him! The only restriction God gave to Satan was, "Don't kill him."

You know the story: Job lost almost everything. All ten of his children were killed, and most of his servants, livestock, and property were deceased and destroyed by thieves and natural disasters within hours. Amazingly, Job refused to blame the God he loved and trusted. As a matter of fact, Job's response looked like this: "Then Job arose, tore his robe, and shaved his head; and fell to the ground and worshiped. And he said: 'Naked I came from my mother's womb, and naked shall I return there. The Lord gave, and the Lord has taken away; Blessed be the name of the LORD.' In all this, Job did not sin nor charge God with wrong."[7] God trusted that Job wouldn't curse Him when Satan attacked. Job's response reminds me of the prodigal son returning home to his father's house, willing to be a servant. Job trusted the nature of God and refused to blame God, rejecting the lie that God was not good.

When Job became afflicted with bodily sores, his wife did not share the same point of view as her husband, saying, "Do you still hold fast to your integrity? Curse God and die!"[8] This woman had suffered all the same losses right next to her husband. But now, as she watched her husband's body become afflicted, she became undone. Resolute, Job wasn't moved by her words. He responded, "You speak as one of the foolish women speaks. Shall we indeed accept good from God, and shall we not accept adversity?"[9] Scripture records that throughout the entire situation, Job never sinned with his lips.

That sure is a lot to take in. The trauma from the circumstances is overwhelming to process. Job's wife, enmeshed in her own grief, couldn't come alongside her husband's stance in faith once she watched him covered in painful boils. Even those closest to us won't know what we go through when we suffer and experience loss, no matter how close they are.

***

The warrior wanted to quit and give up. *I don't want to be strong,* she thought; *I'm tired.* But her years of training and discipline whispered back, "You will persevere," and she took a deep breath and squared her shoulders. Thick forest brush surrounded her, and she'd been walking alone for far too long. She was forced to stop when her hair got caught in some low-hanging branches. Glimmers of open skies peeked through the overgrowth so she could tell a clearing lay ahead. She didn't know how far she had to go to reach the clearing, but she continued to bushwhack her way through the thicket.

She thought about what the King told her—how the journey was more about her mind and thoughts. She considered how she would need to overcome these challenges in order to navigate the terrain. When she became overwhelmed with the tedious task of creating her own trail, she started to whisper encouragement to herself, "You can do this. You are a seasoned warrior. The King chose *you...*" She felt awkward at first but noticed how empowered she felt when she said the words out loud. Rather than giving in to the fatigue of the now-familiar inward battle, the warrior kept going.

She squatted to push away some of the overgrown brush blocking her entrance into the clearing and stepped out of the tangled mess to freedom from the darkness that had surrounded her.

Familiar sounds welcomed her. Critters scurried, birds chirped, and a breeze blew gently. The sun shone brightly upon her skin as she discovered a more defined trail to follow.

Hope washed over her.

Over time, my perspective changed. Thank God Almighty, my perspective changed! It didn't change because I forced it to. It didn't change because my prayers were answered—it changed when I finally became willing to look in the mirror and address my thoughts accordingly.

I took time to think about what I was thinking about—to let go of old negative thought patterns and replace those thoughts with the truth, even if I didn't understand. When I gave up my right to understand, the peace that surpasses understanding came and guarded my heart and mind.[10]

In addition to my mirror self-talk, I decided to start each day with gratitude and reflect on the blessings I could partake in. I am more naturally inclined to complain and have coffee while brewing my negative thoughts. Being thankful became key in adapting to life with vision loss.

It helped me see.

I'm a bookkeeper by trade, and I welcomed getting back to the familiarity of doing something I'd done since I had started bookkeeping in high school—bank reconciliations. I sat at the table, computer in front of me, eye patch on, pen in hand. And I couldn't tell when my pen would hit the paper. I wanted to cry in protest about how unfair this was. When I was strong enough to return to the kitchen, I fried an egg in a white-coated pan, and I couldn't see the separation between the egg and the pan to know when to flip the egg. My depth perception was way off. When I went to paint pottery, as I had been doing for years, I couldn't tell when my brush was hitting my piece for the fine-lined details. These were all things I had once taken advantage of, and all things I knew I didn't need to give up, but now I would have to adjust for them. So, instead of complaining about what I couldn't do, I chose to be thankful for doing things I had previously taken for granted, even when tears filled my eyes.

I make the choice every day on how I will direct my thoughts and guide my own perspective. Choosing to be thankful takes time. Complaint-filled thoughts still threaten to drown my gratitude in selfish regret, but I have discovered that once I choose to be thankful in one area, the attitude of thankfulness overflows into others.

God's grace—His unmerited, undeserved favor—doesn't always make sense to us, nor does it bring us the outcome we desire. We need reminders about how we can't possibly always know what's best and how life provides opportunities for lessons we need to learn on our journey. We can't see outside of time. We can't know how what we endure now as a "momentary, light affliction" (which feels enduring and heavy) works for us "a far more exceeding and eternal weight of glory."[11]

There are moments in life we may not understand when we are going through them, but God's grace makes a difference. Our circumstances blind us at times from seeing God's grace because the pain feels unfair—times when everything that is happening around us and the agony of facing our situations alone feels impossible. But we aren't alone. We are never alone, and the grace God has given us strengthens us to walk through less-than-ideal circumstances while teaching us lessons we couldn't otherwise have learned.

THE GRACE GOD HAS GIVEN US STRENGTHENS US TO WALK THROUGH LESS-THAN-IDEAL CIRCUMSTANCES WHILE TEACHING US LESSONS WE COULDN'T OTHERWISE HAVE LEARNED.

In times past, when the terrain had been less challenging, her thoughts wandered to her never-ending to-do lists or the constant replay of mistakes she felt she had made in life. Here, instead, she embraced the serenity of the moment. She welcomed the quietness and did not struggle to fill it. She continued on the trail and heard large waterfalls thundering ahead.

The trail widened, and she noticed the King walking alongside her. Surprised and thankful to see Him, she considered telling Him all she had learned about herself and how she would never falter in her faith again. Her thoughts were interrupted as she tripped over some tree roots.

She glanced over at Him—He was indescribable, so tall and majestic. He moved with grace, but every step was also mighty and powerful. His countenance shone, and the folds of His garment released light as He moved. She could have stared at Him forever. He was so strong and peaceful, content and yet aware. He looked back at her with a twinkle in His eyes, and His smile made her feel like she mattered most to Him—like she was the only person who ever existed. She didn't want this moment to end.

Another root impeded her progress, and the King held her arm as she steadied herself. "You never miss anything," she said, and His eyes agreed as they met hers. She kept His pace, or maybe He kept hers. Nonetheless, they continued on the trail until the waterfall came into view. Without speaking, they paused to watch the magnificent cascade plummeting to the rocks below, sending enormous clouds of mists upward, swirling in the wind.

He took her hand, and together, they were lost in the sights and sounds of the majestic display. His voice spoke with the water, "You have endured so much, dear one. Think about how far you have come! You are walking in truth and understand the power of My grace." She kept looking at the falls, taking in both His words and the grandeur of the rushing water.

"I want to live for You," she answered. "I mean, *really* live for You. I don't want to go back to the rush of the pace I used to keep. I was too busy for my own good. I treated my duties for You as a 'to-do' list and not as an expression of my devotion." Her voice shook with the rawness of her confession, but He squeezed her hand, and His strength flowed into her. "I don't want to lose what I've learned."

The King put His arm around her back and walked her in front of Him, then turned her to face Him as He grasped both her hands firmly and said, "You don't have to go back to all the busyness. There is no need to keep the pace you once kept. When you remember truth, you will see grace increase in your life."

She looked back at Him, confused.

He continued, "Grace enables you to do things you couldn't do on your own. Grace gives you the power to live for me." She nodded a little in agreement. "There isn't anything you can do to earn My grace—it is My gift to you. You access it by faith. So, use the same faith you received when you acknowledged Me, became My child, and entered My service to access grace every day. Grace to do life with Me and for Me, even when you can't see Me or feel Me."

Wide-eyed, she responded, "Really?"

He smiled and tightened His grip on her hands, "YES! Really."

She needed to look away from Him. "What's the matter?" He asked as she freed her hands from His.

"I've wasted a lot of time. I was so busy trying to prove my love to You that I missed all You've been trying to give me and teach me for years. For decades, if I'm honest. Time I can't get back. I feel foolish."

"Many in My service are caught in these same mindsets. They work themselves to exhaustion, trying to earn the very things I freely give them. All you need can be accessed through your faith in Me. My sweet one, you didn't know how strong you were until you came on this path you never would have chosen for yourself."

She nodded, and they started to walk again.

The waterfalls were now behind them, and the tree cover thickened. Walking in peace enabled her to remember the truth about herself more easily. She wanted to serve her King more than ever. His voice, barely a whisper, said, "It's time ... it's time for you to see."

ENDNOTES

1. Google search this topic, and you will find many corroborating reports and articles. Specifically, see *How to Manage Your 40,000 Negative Thoughts a Day and Keep Moving Forward* by Sarah Lambersky. Published October 16, 2013 © 2013 Financial Post. https://financialpost.com/entrepreneur/three-techniques-to-manage-40000-negative-thoughts accessed on April 9, 2023.
2. John 1:17, NKJV.
3. See 2 Corinthians 10:5, NKJV.
4. Philippians 4:8, NIV.
5. Jeremiah 29:11, NKJV.
6. Psalm 139:17-18, TPT.
7. Job 1:20-22, NKJV.
8. Job 2:9, NKJV.
9. Job 2:10, NKJV.
10. See Philippians 4:7, NKJV.
11. See 2 Corinthians 4:17-18.

PART
2

FULFILLMENT

"... your faith has healed you."
MATTHEW 9:22 NIV

"Daughter, **your faith** has healed you.
Go in peace and be freed from your suffering."
MARK 5:34 NIV

"Rise and go; **your faith** has made you well."
LUKE 17:19 NIV

"Receive your sight; **your faith** has healed you."
LUKE 18:42 NIV

"O woman, great is **your faith!**
Let it be to you as you desire."
MATTHEW 15:28 NKJV

"Go, for **your faith** has healed you."
MARK 10:52 NLT

" And He (Jesus) did not do many miracles there
because of their **lack of faith.**
MATTHEW 13:58 NIV

NOTE: AUTHOR EMPHASIS ON ALL VERSES

CHAPTER 6

THE MOVEMENT OF FAITH

"Behold Jesus—He grows our faith."
PASTOR MATTHEW MEDICK

They walked on in silence; the warrior felt a lightness to her steps she'd never known before. She felt like skipping! *Skipping?* She couldn't remember even skipping as a kid. Her life had always been about responsibilities and dealing with the fears that accompanied them. Immediately, her mind returned to duty. She felt foolish for skipping. The weight of her responsibilities brought the familiar heaviness back, and her mood began to dampen.

Some tricky footwork brought her attention back to the present. She navigated her way through overgrown roots, uneven ground, and fallen branches. She stepped through a rock scramble and saw a wooden ladder implanted into the terrain she needed to embark upon next.

Now, that's a sight to see.

She'd lost sight of the King but knew the drill at this point. She'd see Him when she needed to see Him.

So here she was alone, alone with the ladder and her thoughts.

She wished she'd had someone to send on ahead of her to test the sturdiness. She'd been on these types of ladders before and never was a fan. She also knew the longer she thought about it, the less likely she was to do it.

After pacing back and forth at the base of the ladder for an undisclosed amount of time, she took a deep breath and stepped on the first rung.

One, two, three, she counted each rung but decided she was better off thinking about something to distract her from what she was doing rather than focusing on it. She forced herself to think back to the conversation she just had at the waterfall.

She was never good at remembering words; she remembered moments by feeling. Feeling strength, feeling sorrow, feeling she needed to work hard—work hard, well, that conversation certainly changed the way she needed to look at working hard; she remembered feeling the grief of that realization hitting her. And then the exuberance of wanting to skip—*what was that all about?*

She made it to the top of the ladder. She let out a deep breath and sigh of relief as she stepped away from the ladder she wanted to forget about. However, once focused on what lay before her, she considered turning around and climbing back down. The trail narrowed significantly alongside the bulging rock of the mountain. Hoping this section wouldn't stay this way for long, she pressed on.

The warrior looked up, trying not to panic. She lost her footing where wet, slippery leaves covered the trail. That small misstep sent her cascading ungracefully down the bank of a steep slope, where she landed with her armor caught, and she found herself wedged tightly between two tree trunks.

She struggled to free herself, but the more she struggled, the more tightly the trees pressed against her thick armor, and she could not budge. *I need help,* she realized, now aware she could not escape from her efforts alone. A feeling she did not like. *How long will I be stuck here? What if an enemy comes? Why wasn't I more careful? What if ...?* Her mind spun with scenarios, each ending with bad news.

"I need help," she whispered, "I cannot do this on my own. Please help."

It wasn't even a prayer in her mind. It felt more like a desperate confession of defeat, but the King had heard her cry. He was waiting for her to ask. Though she was unaware, but before she ever fell, the King had dispatched a company of people she did not know to arrive at exactly this moment. Within seconds of her request, she heard the rustling of leaves.

She held her breath to hear better and strained to see what was coming and from where. Was it friend or foe? Should she cry out or be silent and hope they passed by without notice? She was hopelessly stuck. Helplessly stuck. She looked up to the heavens and said, "It's up to You," and prepared herself to meet whatever would happen next.

Throughout the trial with my eye, weeks turned into months, sitting on the couch every Sunday while my family attended church. Once my strength returned and the eye infection itself had resolved, I could go to church, but I couldn't go to church either. The unknowns of being around a group of people seemed too uncertain for me. The energy to engage with people and answer their questions or handle their (well-meant) platitudes was more than my emotional capacity allowed. Instead, I told my family members to stop taking turns on Sundays for who would stay home with me to administer my eye drop schedule, and I learned to do so myself. I longed for fellowship yet remained too scared to step out. *What if people reject me for how my eye looks?*

I stopped wearing my trendy eye patches after the second cornea transplant. My eye needed light for healing. Four surgeries in seven months not only left my eye misshapen, but I lost the entire iris—the part of the eye that makes it recognizably yours. It is the personality of the eye that sparkles when you are up to mischief, seems clouded when you are in grief, reflects depth and warmth and understanding. The iris reflects the soul, and without it, there is nothing but a gaping hole. Naked and exposed ...

Every glance in the mirror was a fresh reminder. I was in mourning—deeply grieving the change, wrestling with what had been lost—no, *stolen*! I was grappling with whether or not I would ever look or feel normal again. I continued to struggle with how I looked. Over time, I resolved to step out slowly and started to meet with friends one-on-one, and only with people whom I thought I could trust to *accept* the new me. Responses varied. Some completely ignored the situation, while others gently asked if I would be okay with them looking closer at my eye. Some wanted to hear the story and how I really felt; others looked pitifully at me. I tried to follow and gauge the responses. Exhausted, I concluded I needed to accept myself first before expecting others to. I eventually settled my soul to accept unknown reactions from others and decided to return to church. Within weeks, messages on faith stirred up questions I pondered in further study. Intrigued and slightly annoyed, I read about when the disciples asked Jesus to increase their faith. Over and over again, I read through Jesus' response. I read through different versions of the same scriptures and meditated on what I read.

I CONCLUDED I NEEDED TO ACCEPT MYSELF FIRST BEFORE EXPECTING OTHERS TO.

Jesus shared two parables. One is about how, with faith the size of a mustard seed, we can speak to a mulberry tree to uproot and move into the sea, and it will obey. The other parable is a story of a servant and a master. The servant must serve the master before sitting down to eat and should not expect to be praised for doing the work expected of him. We, too, are servants of Christ and, therefore, should not expect special praise for doing what's expected of us.[1] We are expected to use our faith.

The first parable gave the lesson on how using faith—even a tiny amount—could make the impossible possible. The second parable taught us to know our role and do what's expected of us. Jesus didn't hand the disciples more faith; He told them to use their faith.

All this time, I thought my faith had been broken or missing. I discovered I didn't lack faith; I had to use my faith. The crisis uncovered my unbelief from years of disappointments, which left me confused and anxious. Desperate for understanding, I recognized how I tried to earn grace by my works instead of freely receiving the gift from God. Suffering invited the opportunity to get my faith unstuck.

In other words, to become unstuck, I had to first understand my seed of faith was still there. I had buried it in disappointment and tried to fertilize it with my good works. Suffering handed me the shovel to dig it out.

Pastor Matt shared in a sermon, *Traits of Faith from Hebrews 11*.[2] He spoke about Old Testament people, like you and me, who faced challenges in life while seeking God's help and direction. Let's take a look at them:

- **Abel** used his faith to offer God a sacrifice, which God accepted and put him in right standing with God. Abel used his faith to live righteously. *I can use my faith to live righteously.*

- **Enoch** walked in fellowship with God for over three hundred years. Enoch did not experience death since God translated him. Enoch's testimony showed how his life of faith pleased God. *I can share my testimony.*

- **Noah** obeyed God and built an ark as an act of faith. His faith, obedience, and fear of the Lord made him an heir of righteousness. *I can obey God.*

- **Abraham** obeyed God. God called him to go out to the place he would receive as an inheritance, and in faith, he went with no idea where he was going. *When God speaks to me, I can step out and do what He says.*

- **Sarah** conceived and bore a child when she was far too old to do so. She exercised her faith to trust an impossible promise. *I can't have faith where I don't believe God is good. I can trust His promises.*

- **Isaac** spoke blessings over Jacob and Esau concerning the future. *I can speak blessings over others.*

- **Jacob** spoke a blessing over his grandsons, both the sons of Joseph, and worshiped God by faith in humility as he approached death. *I can humbly worship God.*

- **Joseph** lived with vision, and as he prepared to die, he cast vision. *I can use my faith to cast vision.*

- **Moses** was hidden for three months; his parents' faith rose, and they did not give in to the fear of present danger. In faith, **Moses** later led the people of Israel away from captivity despite all the plagues surrounding them. *As I walk in faith, I don't have to fear even when in danger or surrounded by adversity.*

- **Jericho's** walls fell down after seven days because God's people obeyed His instructions by faith. *I can obey God's instructions.*

- **Rahab**, the harlot, did not perish with those who were unbelieving. By faith, she received the Hebrew spies with peace, saving them and showing us salvation. *I can use my faith to believe unto salvation.*

These men and women lived by faith to accomplish great things with and for God. We may not need to build an ark or march around the walls of our cities for seven days, but we can glean great lessons of truth to apply today. Ordinary people like you and me fill the halls of the faith in Hebrews 11.

How do the lessons from these Old Testament heroes of faith have any bearing on how we live now? What does it even mean to use our faith to live righteously? Is this another list of do and don't, right and wrong? To live by faith, we must first believe in <u>who</u> we place our faith in. We put our faith in medical doctors for healthcare, lawyers for legal counsel, CPAs for tax advice—we trust and believe in people who are educated in their craft.

To live by faith in God requires trust and relationship. If we look to the Bible for a set of rules to follow in pursuit of God, we miss all He came to give us. God created us for a relationship with Himself built upon faith and trust. Once my relationship is established, I can glean from God's Word as the standard of truth to uphold my life. Let's remember the law came through Moses, and then Jesus came to fulfill the law and bring us grace and truth. Grace and truth aren't gifts we hang up for display at Christmas and Easter; grace and truth are tools for our daily lives. The truth is God created us for relationship, and we use our faith to approach and live out this relationship. When we understand who we are to God, we can also see who God is to us. We don't need to live like the prodigal son— reckless, selfish, and needlessly squandering our lives, nor do we

WHEN WE UNDERSTAND WHO WE ARE TO GOD, WE CAN ALSO SEE WHO GOD IS TO US.

need to work tirelessly to live righteously in our own strength like the elder brother. Living righteously becomes an overflow of our ongoing relationship with God, and He provides the grace—our superpower—to do so.

When we commune with God, we learn righteous ways of living and discover what He calls us to do with our lives and how to handle the circumstances we face. Noah built the Ark, Moses stretched his rod, and the Israelites marched around the city and blew their trumpets. Relationship provides instruction, and trust enables us to obey. Obeying God isn't about following some harsh taskmaster in the sky to ruin our fun. Obeying God opens the door for divinity to meet with humanity and bring forth purpose in our lives.

A twig snapped, and there was the sound of voices speaking in a tongue she did not know, but her heart was unafraid. In her spirit, she knew they were friendly. She discerned they, like her, were also servants of the King, and relief flooded her soul.

As soon as they saw her, they rushed to where she was trapped, and two supporting her upper body and two grabbing her legs; they pushed her upward to where the trunks widened and grew apart and lifted her free. Gently, they helped her sit down, and one looked her over with medical skill, checking her head, arms, and legs. Another gave her water, and one gathered her gear that had sprawled in all directions as she slid down the slope.

Their kindness emboldened her. In her heart, she knew the King and sent them for her. "How could I have doubted You so soon after being in Your presence?" she whispered. *Oh, when will I learn that You see everything!* Her faith grew.

Maybe all of this faith talk and faith walk stuff is new to you like it was to Rahab. A timeless story. I picture Rahab tired of life and how it had always been, and then opportunity literally knocked at her door, and something stirred inside of her. Rahab didn't settle for normal or give into fear; she reached out and found her salvation.

Maybe you, too, my friend, need to start where Rahab did, willing to open the door to the opportunity knocking. "Behold, I'm standing at the door knocking. If your heart is open to hear My voice and you open the door within, I will come in to you and feast with you, and you will feast with Me."[3] Without knowing it, Rahab's radical faith not only made the way for others to find theirs, but she became part of the divine lineage of Jesus Christ.

Maybe your faith experience was more about keeping a list of do's and don'ts. But, you have always known there is something more, and you have a stir inside you similar to Rahab. Friend, your faith is as close as saying the name of Jesus.

If that's you, let's pray right now:

Lord Jesus, I sense you knocking, and I don't know what that even means, but I do trust You are kind. So, by faith, I'm choosing to open the door of my heart to let You in. Please forgive me of my sins and make my heart your dwelling place. In Your name, amen.

Maybe you are more seasoned in your faith. May I encourage you to share your testimony with others? Use the circles you are in to share the goodness of God. I also caution you to use wisdom and be prudent in doing so. You may have to invite your coworker to coffee in order to share effectively while respecting the boundaries of your job. If your children are grown, reach out to the younger parents in your circles, offer them hope, speak a blessing over them and their children, and cast vision for their future. We are never meant to journey alone, and one seemingly small act of faith on your part may help someone around you get their faith unstuck.

ENDNOTES

1. See Luke 17:5-10.
2. Teaching given by Pastor Matt Medick January 2023; used with permission. See Hebrews 11:4-31 for the 11 faith examples mentioned here.
3. Revelation 3:20, TPT.

CHAPTER 7

PRACTICAL PRINCIPLES OF FAITH

*"Faith is deliberate confidence in the character of God
whose ways you may not understand at the time."*
OSWALD CHAMBERS

How do we even attempt to find God when we are hurting and wounded by life? Religion keeps us working toward the impossible task of presenting ourselves perfectly to God. Yet, God knew we would both suffer and struggle. The last thing we want to think about is figuring out how to pull ourselves together enough to approach God.

When the disciples asked Jesus who would be the greatest in the kingdom of heaven, Jesus responded by calling a little child to Himself, "... Truly I tell you, unless you change and become like little children, you will never enter the kingdom of heaven. Therefore, whoever takes the lowly position of this child is the greatest in the kingdom of heaven. And whoever welcomes one such child in My name welcomes Me."[1]

Jesus reminds us to come to Him *like a child*. We start by coming to Him, even when, or I should say, especially when we feel wounded and broken by life. The Aramaic translation of childlike is **Talitha**, which means "wounded lamb."[2] Jesus invites us to come to Him like wounded lambs because He knew how the circumstances of our lives would sometimes leave us wounded and stuck.

Thankfully, Jesus gave us valuable instructions in His response to the question, instructions to apply to our life of faith. Let's look at another translation to provide more understanding:

"He called a little child and set him before them, and said, 'I assure you and most solemnly say to you, unless you repent [that is, change your inner self—your old way of thinking, live changed lives] and become like children [trusting, humble, and forgiving], you will never enter the kingdom of heaven. Therefore, whoever humbles himself like this child is greatest in the kingdom of heaven.'"[3]

We can come to God in our brokenness, with our wounds, heartache, and questions. He is safe for us to trust, strong enough for us to humble ourselves, and forgave us first so we, too, can forgive others. These verses are a good scrub brush for our faith and an extra push we need to get our faith unstuck.

Let's talk about what Jesus pointed out in Matthew 18.

- Repent

And become like little children who are:

- Trusting

- Humble

- Forgiving

Repenting is "the act of changing one's mind" and to "change your inner self—your old way of thinking."[4] In order to repent, we must acknowledge the need for a change in our current mindset. Repentance creates the space where we can change the direction of our minds.[5]

Trusting is connected to our relationship. We trust our banking system when we bring our money to set up accounts. We trust each other to follow the rules of driving at stoplights. We trust our intimate relationships with our secrets and true selves. When we come to God, we find we can trust Him—even when we do not understand His timing or His ways.

Humbling ourselves can be so challenging. Naaman was the commander of the army of Aram and had leprosy. His wife's servant, a young girl from Israel, told him about the prophet in Samaria who could heal. Naaman showed up at the prophet Elisha's door with his horses and chariots and was surprised when Elisha sent a messenger to answer and tell him to wash himself in the Jordan seven times and he would be healed!

Understandably, this made Naaman angry. He took it as disrespect that Elisha did not come out to him but sent a messenger. His expectations were totally blown when the prophet of God did not stand, call on the name of Yahweh, wave his hand over the spot, and cure him. The Jordan River was filthy—not a place where a commander of the army bathes. He left enraged, unwilling to follow the messenger's instruction.

I admit, I more than likely would have been upset like Naaman. He was a highly regarded, valiant soldier who had already yielded his pride just to take the word of a servant girl and make the trip to see Elisha—who didn't even have the courtesy to come outside and meet him!

His servants had better sense. They confronted him, "If the prophet had asked you to do some great thing, wouldn't you have done it? Instead, he sent you a message to do something simple: wash yourself and be cleansed."

What brave servants to speak up to Naaman! Naaman had to humble himself to accept the way the instructions came and follow them against his own initial judgment. I don't know if it was hope or desperation, but Naaman went down to the river and dipped himself seven times—even though it made absolutely no sense. The result? He was healed! His leprosy was gone, and his skin was as clean and clear as a young boy. He exercised faith he didn't even know he had, and in that act, He met God and received grace.[6]

Humbling ourselves doesn't require any sense of humiliation, but it usually requires us to let go of our desire to control and understand. When we humble ourselves to God's ways, the benefits always outweigh the cost. Just remember Naaman.

Forgiveness is so hard but so necessary. Pastor and author R.T. Kendall writes, "The most natural tendency in the world is to want to get even when someone has offended you. It is as natural as eating or sleeping, and it is instinctual. Jesus is telling us to do something that is not natural: totally forgiving people—sometimes those closest to us—for wrongs they do to us."[7]

Kendall continues, "Total forgiveness is painful. It hurts when we kiss revenge goodbye. It hurts to think that the person is getting away with what they did and nobody else will ever find out."[8]

Jesus addresses the topic of forgiveness in ways to use and grow our faith. In *The Lord's Prayer,* He states the necessity of forgiveness, "And when you pray, make sure you forgive the faults of others so that your Father in heaven will also forgive you."[9]

I want to be forgiven completely, so I need to forgive completely. Many times in my life, when circumstances raged and justice should have been done because someone did me wrong, God appeared silent. I would declare the wrongdoings committed against me from the rooftops. I freely cast judgment and tried to stand in the place of judge and jury towards anyone who wronged me. Then, I learned years ago how forgiveness is a choice, not a feeling!

When we forgive, we are letting go and letting God be the judge and jury, and even if we never see how He will handle it, He will handle it. We will all stand and give an account of our lives one day and all the careless words and deeds we committed. When we forgive, we are free from the offense and the heaviness of it. "When I truly and totally forgive, I have crossed over into the supernatural—and achieved an accomplishment equal to any miracle."[10]

> "WHEN I TRULY AND TOTALY FORGIVE, I HAVE CROSSED OVER INTO THE SUPERNATURAL—AND ACHIEVED AN ACCOMPLIHSMENT EQUAL TO ANY MIRACLE."
>
> R.T. KENDALL

Jesus knew we would struggle at times and need to forgive the same offense over and over again:

"So watch yourselves. If your brother or sister sins against you, rebuke them; and if they repent, forgive them. Even if they sin against you seven times in a day and seven times come back to you saying 'I repent,' you must forgive them."[11]

This verse comes from the same passage of scripture discussed previously. The disciples' response to Jesus's instruction on how frequently we are to forgive: "The apostles said to the Lord, 'Increase our faith!'"[12] How interesting that they asked for more faith regarding the topic of forgiveness!

Forgiveness encompasses all of the traits we've been talking about from Matthew 18—having faith like a child, repenting and changing our way of thinking, trusting in the act of forgiving, humbling ourselves, and letting go.

Jesus isn't expecting us to do something He didn't have to do. He modeled forgiveness. As He hung on the cross, Jesus said, "Father, forgive them, for they do not know what they are doing."[13]

We are taking control of our own lives when we choose to forgive. We find freedom and create a path to healing. Forgiveness isn't just an important spiritual practice we need to implement as part of our lifestyle of faith; it is beneficial to our overall mental, physical, and emotional health as well. Sometimes, the person we need to forgive most is ourselves.

Johns Hopkins Medicine reports, "Studies have found that the act of forgiveness can reap huge rewards for your health, lowering the risk of heart attack; improving cholesterol levels and sleep; and reducing pain, blood pressure, and levels of anxiety, depression and stress. And research points to an increase in the forgiveness-health connection as you age."[14]

Our feelings may protest our decision to forgive. We may need to forgive the same offense multiple times every day, but over time, our feelings will catch up, and we will know we are on our path to forgiveness, especially when we finally stop talking about it.

When we approach Jesus like children, we don't worry about checking all the boxes. Jesus is the Good Shepherd who shepherds our souls. When we come broken, confused, and wounded, He doesn't just want to put our broken pieces back together; He wants to make something beautiful with our brokenness.

PLATES OF FAITH

We are professional plate spinners. We spin our plates of marriage, family, our kid's education, our careers, aging loved ones, our faith, our kids' faith …

What happens when one of those plates falls? Another plate will usually follow until we end up with a pile of broken plates. We respond in fear and scramble to try and find a way to get any remains of the broken plates to spin again. But what if God wants to take the pieces and make something new?

A Japanese Art form called Kintsugi restores broken ceramic pottery. The word *Kintsugi* means "golden rejoining" and refers to acknowledging flaws, embracing change, and restoring an object with newfound beauty. The method uses a lacquer dusted with gold or other metals to repair cracked, chipped, or broken dishes. "The idea behind Kintsugi is to highlight—rather than hide—an object's flaws, making them beautiful instead of unsightly. The results are gorgeous."[15] When we approach God as wounded lambs with our childlike faith, God wants to restore us with a newfound beauty.

On May 6, 2023, it was 296 Days after the second cornea transplant. Something in my eye felt wrong, and my eye looked wrong—even for me. Two of my kids, who had been traveling separately and returned home on different days earlier in the week, had the same reaction when they looked at me. "Mom, you should call the doctor; your eye doesn't look good." They confirmed to me what I had already been feeling. I didn't want to overreact when things didn't feel normal; I didn't trust my own judgment. I needed the audible from those who were used to seeing me every day.

"Mrs. Devernoe, your body is trying to reject the transplant. We need to come up with a treatment plan."

As I took in the information from the doctor, I felt emotionally exhausted. Staying busy with springtime events helped initially to keep me from wallowing, but something about sitting in my same spot on the couch and the unsettling prognosis brought it all back.

The enemy of my soul came and gave me a big shove to knock me backward. I expected to feel the familiar darkness of fear and uncertainty, similar to when the issues started in December 2021. Memories from the past sixteen months swirled around in my mind. Pain, longing to be well, and the nag of striving to find my normal surrounded my thoughts.

I went for a walk, and with each step I took, I realized things were different. Ultimately, I was different. I had learned to trust in the good character of God. Even though I wanted to retreat and hide from another trial with my eye, I knew I didn't have to. Habit made me want to shut down and whine. Truth told me I could not. My faith required me to contend.

―――――――――――――

The warrior sat there surrounded by those who had rescued her, shame began to flood her mind and soul, replacing the gratitude she had just felt toward Her King. She scolded herself mentally, spiraling down the slippery slope of negative thoughts. *How could I have been so stupid? I should have seen that spot in the trail. I shouldn't have slipped. I shouldn't be here. I failed. I'm a failure. I'm a burden. The King must be so disappointed in me.*

The ease with which her thoughts turned an accident into a definition of herself as a failure was unnerving.

Noticing her change in demeanor, the heaviness that blanketed her, and the total defeat in her eyes, one of her rescuers knelt beside her. He looked into her eyes, face to face, and she couldn't meet his gaze. Shame cascaded over her as she stifled the tears filling her eyes, and pain squeezed her heart. To her surprise, she heard him whisper in her language, "Look at me." There was such a tenderness and compassion in his voice. She braced herself and looked up. The others faded into the distance as they locked eyes. All she saw was deep concern and compassion. There was no judgment, no pity, no disappointment, anger, or frustration.

The fellow warrior cupped her face in his hands and said, "I know what you are feeling. It's normal to feel this way. Feel it, acknowledge it, and let it go. You are not a failure. You are not a burden. Get back up and keep going. Forgive yourself. Hold your head high, and know we are here for you. We were sent here by Him for you. You are never alone." And then he embraced her.

His words shocked her, and his embrace was exactly what she needed. The tears threatened to pour over as she let herself receive the embrace. He gently pulled away, and extending his arms, he pulled her to her feet. The others put her pack onto her back and adjusted her armor in place. As they turned to leave, a woman pulled a pin from her pocket and placed it on the warrior's chest. "To remind you that you are never alone," she said. Again, the warrior's eyes swam with tears as she watched the others return from where they had come.

She stood there processing the words and the feelings they had stirred up. She realized she had never looked at herself like that. When she pictured herself, it was usually with a harsh and criticizing eye. *That's what made me such a good warrior,* she rationalized. Yet maybe this is what the King had been trying to teach her all along. She thought, *When He looks at me, He looks at me with love. Even when I fall and fail and mess up. He still loves me. He forgives me. He dusts me off and says, "Keep going."*

This was so foreign to her. *Why? How can He, how can others, how can people love me when I mess up?* And the truth came gently to her soul, *because love that is earned is no love at all.*

The dense clouds that had overshadowed her heart began to break, and she heard the bird's song flitting through the forest and noticed the smell of fresh pine all around her. The wind blew gently, caressing her cheeks, and she knew she had a decision to make.

She could keep going, show up on this trail, and not let the failure and fear define her. She could forgive herself for what she perceived as failure and press on to finish the path set before her. Or she could let the shame and condemnation, which felt so natural and even justified, wrap around her and cause her to retreat. Self-sabotage, or self-forgiveness. That was the choice before her.

With that, the warrior made up her mind. She would be no coward. Funny how choosing love and forgiveness requires bravery—more bravery than wading into a life-threatening battle head-on. It would be a fight, but she was willing—finally—to fight for the right thing. She took a deep breath and whispered to the King, "Thank You for helping me. Thank You for loving me. I receive that love. When I look at myself, help me look through Your eyes of tender love, forgiveness, and compassion. I give You these feelings of shame and condemnation. Please fill me with the strength to overcome my fears of failing again and help me to put one foot in front of the other. Ever climbing, ever moving forward until I reach the end."

She inhaled deeply, welcoming peace, and started her trek back up to the trail. Feeling lighter and full of hope, with a smile on her face.

WE CONTEND

"Beloved, while I was very diligent to write you concerning our common salvation, I found it necessary to write to you exhorting you to *contend* earnestly for the faith which was once for all delivered to the **saints**."[16]

When we contend for something, it is "the meeting of effort by effort, striving against opposition."[17]

I followed the doctor's treatment plan—the schedules of various eye drops, the I.V. steroids, and oral steroids. Now, I needed to follow God's treatment plan—contend.

The context of what we stand against will dictate the way we contend. How do we contend for our faith? We talked earlier in Chapter 5 about the importance of knowing what we are thinking about and how we need to take our thoughts captive. Fear and unbelief attack us in our thoughts, and we cannot sustain a battlefield of thoughts against thoughts.

To stand against the opposition, we need to take the Word of God and declare it out loud, as Nehemiah did. "So I contended with the rulers, and **said**, 'Why is the house of God forsaken?' And I gathered them together and set them in their place."[18]

To stand against our enemy requires that we take our thoughts captive and declare God's Word against the struggle.[19] When we contend, we hold onto what we believe. *Effort by effort. Again and again.*

WHEN WE CONTEND, WE HOLD ONTO WHAT WE BELIEVE.

In response to life circumstances, we are usually too quick to react in the flesh and lie down instead of standing up for our faith.

When we look at the book of Jude for instruction to contend for our faith, let's consider the audience to whom Jude wrote and the context of this short, powerful book. Jude told fellow believers of the Gospel to contend for their faith, for the truth, not what the culture or false teachers were presenting at that time.

Years of Christian clichés, works, and trendy messages which excited my flesh weren't helping to grow my faith. Truth and grace did. The truth of God's Word was revealed to me through learning, listening, and studying the scriptures. I obtained the grace to adhere to God's Word wherein I humble myself and allow the Bible to govern my thoughts and, therefore, my life.

Bible teacher and author Tony Evans says faith is acting like God is telling the truth. God has given us—you and me—amazing promises in His Word. We may have different things we use our faith for, but we can glean reminders from biblical heroes who chose to believe and accomplish amazing things we still remember today! We have our own paths of obedience to follow, our own testimonies to share, and specific people to cast vision to as we bring light onto their paths.

Life creates opportunities for us when we live by faith. To live by faith isn't to live without challenges or problems. Faith isn't just for when we need help with challenges or problems. To live by faith encompasses our daily life and the choices we make.

Ordinary becomes supernatural, mundane becomes exciting, and the impossible becomes possible.

What then defines the extravagant moments of faith throughout scripture lived out by ordinary people like you and me? The difference, or similarity, between us and them is what they chose to believe. What we believe is what we will contend for. Speaking the Word of God over my life, my circumstances, and the anguish in my soul not only enabled me to contend but gave me healthy soil for my faith to grow. Living by faith doesn't require an ability to see because it's an inward knowing of what can't be seen. We are called to walk by faith, not by sight.[20]

As you take steps in your own faith, meditate on this scripture to reflect on what you are hoping for in your life.

*"Now **faith** is confidence in what we **hope** for and assurance about what we do not see."*
HEBREWS 11:1, NIV
EMPHASIS ADDED

ENDNOTES

1. Matthew 18:3-5, NIV.
2. This translation of *talitha* is taken from a verse notation following "little child" inside Matthew 18:3 from *The Passion Translation*. YouVersion: www. *https:// www.bible.com/bible/1849/MAT.18.TPT accessed on June 21, 2023.*
3. Matthew 18:2-4, AMP.
4. Definition of "Repent" taken from *The Amplified Bible,* Matthew 18:3.
5. "What Does the Bible Say About Repentance?" From *www.gotquestions.org* accessed on June 21, 2023.
6. Read 2 Kings 5 for the full account of Naaman's healing.
7. Kendall, R.T. *Total Forgiveness*, Charisma House, 2002.
8. Ibid.
9. Matthew 6:14, TPT.
10. Kendall, R.T. *Total Forgiveness*, Charisma House, 2002.
11. Luke 17:3-4, NIV.
12. Luke 17:5, NIV.
13. Luke 23:34, NIV.
14. *Forgiveness: Your Health Depends on It* © 2023 The Johns Hopkins University, The Johns Hopkins Hospital, and Johns Hopkins Health System, All Rights Reserved. *https://www.hopkinsmedicine.org/health/wellness-and-prevention/forgiveness-your-health-depends-on-it#:~:text=%E2%80%9CIt%20is%20 an%20active%20process,the%20person%20who%20wronged%20you.* Accessed on June 13, 2023.
15. *Kintsugi: The Japanese Art of Finding Beauty in Broken Dishes* by Camryn Rabideau, published on April 17, 2017 © Martha Stewart. All Rights Reserved. *https://www.marthastewart.com/1515372/kintsugi-japanese-art-finding-beauty-broken-dishes accessed on March 8,* 2023.
16. Jude 1:3, NKJV, emphasis added.
17. Contend. *https://www.biblestudytools.com/dictionary/contend-contention/* accessed on March 20, 2023.
18. Nehemiah 13:11, NKJV.
19. See 2 Corinthians 10:4-6.
20. See 2 Corinthians 5:7, NIV.

C H A P T E R 8

CULTIVATE HOPE

*"Hope doesn't go to sleep just because
it's dark outside; it lights a candle and stays up
waiting for the rest of the story."*
BOB GOFF

My breathing became labored, I started to sweat, and my hands were shaking. I just needed to make it through one more store, and I would head home. I worked my way through the crowds, overwhelmed by store displays, and forgot who I was shopping for.

The hustle and bustle of the holiday season invoked my anxiety. After inviting Jesus to calm the storm of anxiety after my second surgery, I noticed I had the courage to <u>feel</u> rather than <u>resist</u> anxiety when it came. Always before, I had viewed anxiety through the lens of thoughts that needed to be taken captive, and entertaining anxiety was disobedience of some kind. I came to realize that this was bad theology and a misapplication of scripture. Anxiety arises when your brain and emotions are overloaded. It happens when there is more to process than you can reasonably assimilate in a given moment. True, anxiety can lead you into a spiral of negative thoughts and limiting beliefs that do, indeed, need to be taken captive. But when your emotions are in turmoil in response to trauma, anxiety is not a sin—it is a symptom that your soul is in distress and needs care.

This was a new paradigm for me. Anxiety wasn't something I could ignore or declare away. Anxiety was an invitation to pause and process what was happening and why. It was an opportunity to shelter beneath the shadow of His wings and find rest for my soul.

Throughout the journey of understanding my faith, I stopped trying to avoid my anxiety when it would stir up. I no longer resented or rejected this part of myself. Enduring suffering, while uncovering my faith, created space to feel my anxiety. Rather than ignoring this lifelong shadow or busying myself into oblivion, I learned to feel every overwhelming moment of it.

Feeling anxiety enabled me to experience healing in a part of myself I'd been trying to shut up like an annoying child. I became vulnerable with myself in ways I hadn't known before. The kind of vulnerability we long for in relationships where we want to be accepted for our truest selves, but feel too scared to let others see.

Similar to seeing more family and friends during the holiday season, by feeling the anxiety, I opened the door to let what felt like an old friend back into my life. You know, one of those relationships where you couldn't really be friends for a sustainable amount of time, but also can't deny how much history you shared?

"The idea of *feeling* your anxiety as a way of finding relief from it can sound counterintuitive or even crazy because it's the exact opposite of everything you've been taught about in our culture. That anxiety is this bad thing, an abnormal disorder you need to manage and ideally get rid of." The author quoted here continued her reflection by sharing how anxiety becomes excess energy trapped in the body from repressed emotions such as sadness, grief, shame, or anger that haven't been processed.[1]

"I'M FEELING"

My family and I love Jim Carey as the Grinch in Dr. Seuss's *How the Grinch Stole Christmas*. He anxiously awaited devastation for the Whos in Whoville after he stole all their precious Christmas gifts and decorations. He watched them valiantly from afar when they awakened to discover their losses. However, when they exited their homes to share the news of their plight together, instead of cries of loss and grief, he heard them sing as they gathered around the city Christmas Tree, holding hands. The Grinch, struck in wonder, proclaimed, "Maybe Christmas doesn't come from a store. Maybe, Christmas, perhaps means a little bit more" and dramatically collapsed in pain, realizing he was *feeling*!

The Grinch had lost hope for what he longed for most: relationship and acceptance from the Whos. Hurt and angry about how they focused more on their crazy, overindulgent Christmas preparation, the Grinch withdrew.

Hope is a key component of our well-being. Without it, we are victims of everything and have no power to influence outcomes or reach into possibilities.

WHERE'S YOUR HOPE?

I hope she gets better. I hope he gets his act together and they don't end up in a divorce. I hope my child does well on their test. I hope the procedure goes as planned. I hope this relationship works out. I hope this diet works ...

We hope for a lot of things and toss the word hope around haphazardly. If we aren't careful, we ride the wave of emotions from our circumstances based on wishful thinking. Whereas biblical hope is not a shallow wishing; it is a confident expectation based upon believing God's promises found in His Word. Where we place our hope affects our overall health, including our mental health.

The relationship between hope and mental health has been a topic of debate for influential thinkers and thought leaders throughout history. Martin Luther celebrated hope and proclaimed, "Everything that is done in this world is done by hope."

Centuries later, Benjamin Franklin influenced the field of psychology with his studies on human behavior. His systematic self-improvement procedure is similar to cognitive behavior therapy used today. Franklin's stance on hope vastly differed from Martin Luther's. Franklin warned, "He that lives upon hope will die fasting."[2]

Today, as a culture, we are more aware of the importance of clinical mental health than ever. In a 2019 clinical trial in Cognitive Behavior Therapy (CBT) on the effects of hope in recovering from anxiety disorders, Matthew W. Gallagher reported, "Hope was a common element and strong prediction of recovery." Furthermore, "the magnitude of these changes in hope were consistent across different CBT protocols and across the four anxiety disorders examined, which underscores the broad relevance of instilling hope as an important factor in promoting recovery during psychotherapy."

The trial looked at individuals with social anxiety disorder, panic disorder, generalized anxiety disorder, and obsessive-compulsive disorder. Results also indicated how therapists working with clients who are stuck should utilize hope as a means to guide their patients toward recovery.[3]

While the results from the study are encouraging, each person needs to determine the focus of their hope for sustainability.

Throughout the crisis with my eye, I traversed the challenges in my faith while hoping everything we tried would restore my vision. Many months later, when doctors told me my body

I CLUNG TO MY NEWLY AWAKENED FAITH, BUT REALIZED I LACKED HOPE FOR MY FUTURE ...

was trying to reject the cornea transplant, I clung to my newly awakened faith, but realized I lacked hope for my future with my eye. My hope had become more about wishful thinking based on my circumstances than about the biblical hope I craved.

My friend, you have journeyed with me in these pages to discover scriptures and biblical truths to uncover my faith. You watched as I sorted through how my works need to be an expression of my faith and not an attempt to earn God's free gift of grace. You witnessed the choice I made over wallowing in self-pity to instead think about what I am thinking about and recognize the power of God's Word to take my thoughts captive. You observed how I uncovered the courage to accept the invitation to my suffering as an opportunity to travel new, unknown, less traveled paths.

How, then, did yet another roller coaster ride of wishful thinking land me back to the start? *I didn't even get to pass GO and collect $200!*

I am disappointed.

I am disappointed with the outcome.

I am disappointed with where I am today, and I haven't a clue how to reach for my tomorrow.

"Why are you cast down, O My soul?
And why are you disquieted within me?
Hope in God, for I shall yet praise Him
for the help of His countenance."

— PSALM 42:5, NKJV

I'm so thankful for the Psalms. David poured out his heart to the Lord in many Psalms. David expressed his truest self before the One he trusted the most. In his challenges, in his failures and shortcomings, David shows us we, too, are safe with an all-loving, all-knowing God.

David cultivated his relationship with the Lord as a young shepherd boy. When the prophet Samuel came to David's home with instructions to anoint the next King of Israel, David's father presented all seven of David's brothers before him. Samuel inquired if Jesse had another son. David, forgotten by his father yet chosen by God, was called in from tending the sheep to come before the prophet. Samuel anointed him as King—a future promise David wasn't seeking or promoting himself for. David's future was sealed with a direct promise from God, but he didn't move out of his father's house that day. He didn't get a scepter and a robe and step into that promise instantaneously. He returned to tending the sheep.

Years later, David was summoned to play his harp for King Saul in an attempt to bring him relief. David did indeed bring the King relief. David, a teenager, was also the only one who had enough courage to take on Goliath, who shouted his challenge along the battlefield from behind the enemy lines against the army of Israel. David slayed Goliath with skills he mastered as a shepherd and won the hearts of many, except King Saul. The King, filled with rage against David's growing popularity, left David with no other option than to flee. So the one Samuel anointed to be Israel's King was now reduced to hiding in caves, fighting for his life against King Saul, whom he loved and served.

Talk about disappointment.

David could have given up on the promise. He could have shaken his fist at God and demanded an explanation. Rather, we see how David addressed his soul—his mind, will, and emotions, to put hope in God throughout varying circumstances in his life. Like David, we can direct our souls to do the same. We need to do what David did, pour out our hearts before the Lord, and exercise our faith to put our hope in God. Hope is never inferior to our faith; it partners with our faith—it is more of an extension of our faith.

To obtain and walk in biblical hope, I needed my journey first to uncover and then to strengthen my faith. So now, I can cross the bridge of faith over to biblical hope.

BENEFITS OF BIBLICAL HOPE

God means for us to have a living, energetic hope. Peter said, "Celebrate with praises the God and Father of our Lord Jesus Christ, who has shown us His extravagant mercy. For His fountain of mercy has given us a new life—we are reborn to experience a *living, energetic hope.*"[4]

Yes, please! When I acknowledge my disappointment to the Lord and direct my hope in Him, I experience living, energetic hope based on God's promises. Rather than wishful thinking about my circumstances, I use my faith to confidently expect good to happen. Hope doesn't see. Hope doesn't have to understand; hope trusts. Hope acknowledges God has a plan, which helps us allow Him to direct our path.[5] Faith is what we are sure of in our hearts right now. Hope is for what our minds believe about the future. When I direct my hope by faith, I also receive the additional benefits of peace sprinkled with joy.

Hope doesn't change our circumstances, but we change in the midst of our circumstances. If someone was able to just tell me what the final outcome would be with my eye, I could have peace going through what I need to go through to get there. Life doesn't work that way. I am, however, willing to let go of my need to understand and release my disappointment. Biblical hope enables me to do so. Peace inevitably comes when we are willing to let go of our need to understand.

I lost my hope when my daughters weren't healed within my timeframe. Life went on, like it always does, and I allowed disappointment to feed my hopelessness. When I needed hope to connect with my faith to believe for healing when I became afflicted, I carried around a monster of hopelessness instead. When we use our faith to hope in the Lord—to trust Him, we don't have to rely on our understanding; we overflow with hope by the power of the Holy Spirit,[6] and we become free to experience peace and walk in joy.

WHAT ANXIETY TAUGHT ME

When the storm calms, we are not only able to see more clearly, but to hear more clearly as well.

Over the years, my attempts to avoid my anxiety made my inner life cluttered and noisy. I needed quiet within me to hear. My anxiety has a voice I need to listen to, but I don't need to live by it. Rather than waste energy trying to quiet the anxiety altogether, I need to listen so I will understand what it's trying to show me. Maybe I need to cry because of a missed opportunity or need to write a letter I will never send to the person who hurt me. Maybe I need to visit the cemetery of my loved one to finally make peace. Maybe I need to forgive myself for mistakes I've made. I can journal, hike, connect with a friend. I can take my anxious thoughts before the Lord, over and over again, as David did in the Psalms when he said, "Whenever my busy thoughts were out of control, the soothing comfort of your presence calmed me down and overwhelmed me with delight."[7]

My heart may not grow three sizes from finally allowing myself to feel my anxiety, but I can allow myself to release the pent-up feelings of my yesterdays safely. Listening to what I am anxious about enables me to direct my soul to hope in the Lord. Doing so enables me to create space to walk in faith without remaining overwhelmed. So, instead of being locked up in the trunk with anxiety in the driver's seat,[8] I can hop in the passenger seat and sing, "Jesus Take the Wheel!"

HEART QUESTIONS

Too often, our own humanity causes us to stop in our tracks in our relationship with God. When we come to a place where we question God, we tell ourselves we shouldn't feel this way and abandon our walk with God.

Throughout scripture, we see how God desires relationship with His people. From the beginning, God has endeavored to communicate with His people. He walked in the cool of the day with Adam and gave detailed instructions to Old Testament heroes of faith, Abraham, Noah, and Moses, to name a few. God spoke to and through Old Testament Prophets and made the way for all mankind when the Messiah and Savior, Jesus Christ, came as fulfillment of the law. Jesus Himself did life with His disciples and close followers and enjoyed fellowship with friends He frequently spent time with and broke bread with.

Questioning is a natural form of communication. God asked His people questions. Jesus asked questions to show others their own hearts. Job asked questions in his suffering, as did Habakkuk when he questioned God's seeming lack of involvement in great times of evil in Judah.

Instead of going to God with our questions, we withdraw and assign His motives and assume His answers. God can handle our questions. When we play out the falsely assigned motives we give to God, we hinder our own well-being.

During Jesus's visit with friends, Martha, Mary, and Lazarus, Martha questioned Jesus, "But Martha became exasperated with finishing the numerous household chores in preparation for her guests, so she interrupted Jesus and said, 'Lord, don't you think it's unfair that my sister left me to do all the work by myself? You should tell her to get up and help me.'

"The Lord answered her, 'Martha, my beloved Martha. Why are you upset and troubled, pulled away by all these many distractions? Mary has discovered the one thing most important by choosing to sit at my feet. She is undistracted, and I won't take this privilege from her.'"9

Martha was "exasperated," and she even "interrupted" Jesus as she told Him what He should do. My girl! But let's look at Jesus's response to her, "Martha, my beloved Martha." What! How beautifully enduring! In my busy household, both exasperations and interruptions happen frequently, and we certainly don't handle them like this. Jesus acknowledged how Martha felt while bringing her correction wrapped gently in His love for her through their relationship.

There will be times when I question, and that's okay. There will also be times to let it all go and rest in trusting in God— when I need to stop questioning and, like Mary, say, "According to Your Word, be it unto me."10 We connect with God with our faith and hope for what He wants to do with our lives—today, tomorrow, and always—even when we don't understand or have the outcome we want. God stands outside of time. Putting our hope in an eternal God who knows our beginning and our end and everything in between and who has promised to work it all out for our good because we love Him grants comfort too incredible to comprehend.

~———————~

The warrior walked on in the seclusion of the forest, contemplating her fall and rescue. She examined her thoughts. She reached out to the King with her unanswered questions without pretending she shouldn't have them. The heat of battle and the engagement of command had always kept her darker thoughts at bay. If she admitted it, she had preferred it that way. She was beginning to see why the King sent her on this leg of her journey alone. It wasn't to isolate her; it was to quiet her mind and replenish her soul. It had slowed her down enough to listen. It had allowed her time to be instead of just to do. Yes, isolation was dangerous for the warrior. It had always led to torturous thoughts and fears, but solitude, she was learning, was beautiful. A gift.

As she walked along, almost without realizing it, a song stirred in her belly, and the melody that sprang forth from her lips was a song of hope. The refrain was pure freedom, unbridled joy in trusting her King, and knowing that anything she would ever endure was in the scope of His care.

She had no idea what lay ahead for her, but she knew she could trust Her King. In that trust, she was safe.

And that safety wrapped her heart in comfort she had never known before.

ENDNOTES

1. "Anxiety Needs to Be Felt to Be Metabolized," by Kli, Efthymia, MA Trauma Specialist, @the.trauma.educator Post on December 4, 2022.

2. "Benjamin Franklin's Other Job: Psychologist," by Rooney, John, posted on May 17, 2022. https://www.realclearhistory.com/articles/2022/05/17/benjamin_franklins_other_job_psychologist_832883.htmlaccessed on May 24, 2023.

3. "Hope is a Key Factor in Recovering From Anxiety Disorders" by Fickman, Laurie, posted October 14, 2019. https://uh.edu/news-events/stories/2019/october-2019/101419-hope-anxiety-gallagher.php accessed on May 24, 2023.

4. 1 Peter 1:3, TPT (author emphasis).

5. See Proverbs 3:5-6, NKJV.

6. See Romans 15:13, NIV.

7. Psalm 94:19, TPT.

8. See Chapter 2 for this illustration.

9. Luke 10:40-42, TPT.

10. See Luke 1:38.

CHAPTER 9

PURPOSE-DEFINING LOVE

"When we open up our eyes to see God's love pursuing us, we find our purpose."
LAURIE DEVERNOE

The warrior trod on. Her new confidence made her feel strong and brave—not about battle, she had always thrived on the battlefield—now she felt brave in *who she was.* She knew she had the favor of the King! *It must be because I have been so faithful,* she thought to herself, and she began to rehearse all the times when she had sacrificed, endured hardship, and stayed true to the King. She thought back to a particular season where she not only carried out her own responsibilities with great skill but also took on caring for other younger, less experienced, less skilled warriors than herself. She engaged them in training and enabled them to grow in the techniques she taught them. When others encountered her trainees, they knew they were *her* students. As a result, she found strength in watching her skills come alive in others. She did these things out of love for Him. Her own position of self-appointment.

She lived by her personal code of honor for so long that it had become a core belief—a belief through which everything that ever happened to her was measured. When she was "good," good things happened to her or for her. When she was "not good," then things did not go well for her until she mended her ways and was "good" again.

She did not believe she was capable of deception by the enemy. She was positive she knew friend from foe. She did not think it was possible that anyone could persuade her affections or cause her to stray from her commission by His Majesty.

—⁓—————⁓—

Peter stretched and relaxed; his belly was full of food. His heart was still glowing from having supper with Jesus and the other disciples. He hummed the hymn they had sung together as they walked out of the house and made their way to the Mount of Olives. He shook his head and shuddered as he thought about one of them betraying Jesus. *I could never do that,* he thought to himself.

As if Jesus had heard his thoughts, He said, "You will *all* fall away because of me, and it will happen tonight ... but once I have risen, I'll go ahead of you and lead the way to Galilee."

"Not me, Jesus!" Peter interrupted in earnest, "Even if every other person walks away from you, I *never* will!"

Jesus looked at Peter, love and compassion in His eyes, "Peter," he said and shook His head gently, "before the rooster crows at dawn—before this night has passed, you will deny me three times."

"No! Even if I have to die with you, I could never deny You, Jesus!" Peter shouted.[1]

───────────────

Jesus knew Peter would deny Him, and Jesus knew when He told Peter that he would do so, Peter wouldn't believe Him. Jesus was aware Peter *wanted* to be strong and loyal—even if it cost him his life. But Jesus also knew Peter would fail despite his intentions.

Then, the crucifixion and the resurrection happened.

───────────────

Dejected and miserable, Peter was out fishing with some of the other disciples. From the shore, a man called out, "Did you catch anything?"

"No!" they answered, "Nothing's biting."

The man on shore laughed and said, "Try casting your net on the other side of the boat ... you'll find some!"

It can't be! Peter's mind rejected the thought. *I saw Him die!* And he went to work moving the net over. Within minutes, it was so full they couldn't draw it in. It was too familiar. *It is Him!* Peter's heart soared. He jumped into the water to make his way to Jesus.

What emotions Peter must have experienced in his swim to the shore! The excitement of possibility and the lingering sting from his denial. While none of the disciples mustered the courage to ask, there was Jesus, cooking and eating fish with them on the shore, as He had done many times before.

"Peter, do you *love* me? More than these?" Jesus asked, pointing to His disciples (*Agape*—self-sacrificing love.)[2]

"Yes, Lord, you know that I *love* You!" Peter answered in earnest. (*Phileo*—brotherly, affectionate love.)[3]

"Then feed My lambs," Jesus said.

"Peter," Jesus looked and asked him again, "Son of Jonah, do you *love* Me?" (Again, *agape*—the kind of love that is intentional, backed with reasoning and spiritual devotion as one loves the Father.)[4]

"Yes, yes, of course I do! You know I *love* You!" Peter replied. (Again, Peter's answer was *phileo*, the kind of love that is filled with camaraderie and familial affection.)[5]

"Tend My sheep," was His answer.

Once more, always going to the heart of the matter, Jesus asked Peter, "Do you *love* Me?" (This time, Jesus did not say *agape*; He used the word *phileo*—the brotherly, affectionate love.)[6]

Peter was grieved that Jesus asked Him a third time.[7]

Why did he grieve?

As Jesus walked him through the same question three times, Peter reinstated his declaration of his love for his Messiah the same number of times he had betrayed him. Why was Peter grieved at the third time Jesus asked him? Was his grief because Jesus had to ask him three times? Was it because he had denied Jesus three times? Or was it because Jesus now asked him using the word *phileo* instead of *agape*—kind of a downgrade? Did the realization of his current ability to love grieve him because he had really hoped he could offer Jesus more? The Bible doesn't tell us.

I won't pretend I understand what was going through Peter's mind or why when Jesus asked him, "Do you *agape* me?" Peter answered, "I *phileo* you." But I do know a little something about what it feels like to feel you are incapable of the passionate, intense dedication you once proclaimed for Jesus on the other side of an identity-crushing, faith-shattering experience.

I believe it is possible Peter thought himself incapable of agape love after his betrayal. For him, agape love was a love Peter no longer believed he possessed.

Then Jesus said something remarkable to him. "Peter, listen, when you were younger, you made your own choices and went where you pleased. But one day, when you are old, others will tie you up and escort you where you would not choose to go— and you will spread out your arms."[8] Imagine Jesus stretching His arms wide, the nail-scars visible to Peter as the weight of this prophecy for how Peter would die and glorify God sank in. Imagine something quickening inside Peter as he thought, *Jesus knows everything. He is right about everything. He had been right about my denial, so He must also be right about this, too!*

Dying like that was not *phileo* love. Jesus was describing *agape* love—Peter's future was *agape* love for God! Imagine the transformation as Jesus' words sunk in. Envision Peter, with his eyes brightened, his shoulders squared, his jaw set, as he embraced Jesus with relief and release.

"Now," Jesus said to Peter, "Follow Me."[9]

Jesus' conversation with Peter redefined Peter's love—a love Peter would need to feed the very sheep Jesus kept asking him about and paving the way for how Peter ministered and taught us in the scriptures.[10] We don't define love. God is love, and He defines love. His love defined Peter. Peter had a choice to walk in it.

WE DON'T DEFINE LOVE. GOD IS LOVE, AND HE DEFINES LOVE.

I can't speak for Peter, but in his shoes, I would have expected punishment, or at least an "I told you so." Instead, Jesus used the circumstances and taught Peter in a way that didn't just educate him—it changed him. One conversation redefined and empowered Peter to love in ways he hadn't before. Jesus released destiny through the words He spoke. Jesus' love will do the same for me and you.

———

The disappointment in the exam room felt tangible at my follow-up appointment regarding the auto-immune response. My surgeon, visibly disheartened, told me the treatments didn't work and my body had indeed rejected the second transplant. He continued to explain that the repair surgery he'd done to hold a loose suture in place a few months prior had failed as well. We agreed another transplant didn't seem feasible at this time and decided to follow up in a few months. I fumbled through scheduling my next appointment and tried to breathe deeply once safely in my car by myself.

Before my body's immune system started rejecting the transplant, I had started to see a little. I could make out names on my phone when I was on a call. They were warped and blurry, but I could *see* them. I could *see* a blurred E on the eye chart, and my hope stirred. At church, I could *see* my pastor's silhouette moving in front of the light blue screen. His legs were as tall as the Marvel character Groot's, but I could still see them!

I followed the doctor's protocols. I uprooted my faith into better soil. I received prayer. I forgave others. I spoke the Word of God over my life and my eye.

What was I doing wrong now?

Impossible, the warrior thought back. That was her first response when the news came. One of her trainees, her star student, fell into the darkness, and no one could tell how much damage had been done. For the longest time, the warrior tried to forget that night. The night that dragged on for weeks, and they wondered what the final outcome would be. Time had been lost, and pain ensued without question, but the uncertainty remained ... *would she be able to fight again, breathe on her own again, or even stand again?* The warrior's emotions were almost too much to handle. *How could this happen to one she trained? How could this happen to her—the one who lingered longer than the others after a training session? The one who arrived early to see if there was anything she could do to get things ready? The one who had become her friend and taught her not to take herself so seriously? How could she have allowed herself to go directly into the darkness alone?*

Then, her thoughts left her student and turned inward. *What would others think when they found out the warrior had trained her?* That was the question that stuck the hardest. *What would others think of her when one of hers fell?*

Why does bad news, trials, and suffering feel like punishment? Why do we immediately think we've done something wrong to deserve the hardships life brings us? There isn't a dividing line when it comes to our natural response to suffering. Even as Bible-reading, Bible-believing Christians, we are quick to look for someone to blame—even God—when the heavy blows of life land upon us.

Peter himself told us, "Beloved, do not think it strange concerning the fiery trial which is to try you, as though some strange thing happened to you; but rejoice to the extent that you partake in Christ's sufferings, that when His glory is revealed, you may also be glad with exceeding joy."[11]

I didn't feel like rejoicing after another failed surgery. I didn't know how to feel, and the people closest to me didn't know what to say. I retreated inwardly and found myself questioning what I had done to deserve this. Questioning of this sort doesn't lead us to faith. Questioning of this sort stirs up jealousy and envy, looking at others' seemingly perfect lives while we are left angry, hurt, and confused.

I had a daily choice to make to let go of questioning. Instead, I reminded myself of God's goodness towards me. I focused my thoughts on scripture regarding healing and held onto God's Word instead of the nagging thoughts.

Then, I remembered a scripture: "Afterward, as Jesus walked down the street, he noticed a man blind from birth. His disciples asked him, 'Teacher, whose sin caused this guy's blindness, his own, or the sin of his parent?' Jesus answered, "Neither. It happened to him so that you could watch him experience God's miracle.'"[12]

Another translation records Jesus' answer like this: "Neither this man nor his parents sinned, but it was so that the works of God might be displayed and illustrated in him."[13] It wasn't the sin of the man that caused him to be blind, nor the sin of his parents. It wasn't sin at all. His ailment, his suffering, was for others to watch him experience God's miracle!

> WE AREN'T BEING PUNISHED WHEN WE SUFFER. OUR SUFFERING IS A SETUP FOR GOD TO MOVE ...

We aren't being punished when we suffer. Our suffering is a setup for God to move in our lives so miraculously that others will see and take notice.

The very next thing Jesus did was to spit on the ground and use His saliva to make clay. Then Jesus scooped that clay up from the dirt pile, smeared it on the man's eyes, and told him to go wash it off in the pool of Siloam.

And the man followed Jesus' instructions and could now see![14]

It has taken the unraveling of me, through heartache, pain, loss, disappointment after disappointment, and failed surgeries, to finally see what I needed to see all along.

Suffering *feels* like punishment. Bad news *feels* like we've been singled out because we have done something wrong. Trial and hardship come upon us in life. Bad things happen to good people. But suffering isn't punishment: suffering is an invitation to see how God wants to take the unique circumstances we endure and use them to give us strength and purpose, ultimately for others. Here, I partake in the miracles His grace offers me every day.

As intimate as Peter was with Jesus, he still didn't experience the full measure of Jesus' heart and intentions toward him until he suffered with the results of his choices—choices he had made with the best of intentions. His grief was not punishment; it was the catalyst that transformed his love from surface to depths beyond comprehension. Our lives are the same. In my anger towards God, in my attitude where I thought I had earned my healing and wrestled with why God had not given it to me yet, God remained the same as He did towards Peter. His response towards us in our suffering is always purpose-defining love. God can't change who He is—we change when we come to know who He is.

My sin, my failures, and my mistakes can't keep me from God's love, even when—especially when I suffer.

ENDNOTES

1. Read Matthew 26 for the full account of this story.
2. Bible Hub. Strong's Concordance. Retrieved from https://biblehub.com/lexicon/john/21-15.htm on February 5, 2024.
3. Ibid.
4. Two Words for Love in John 21:15-17. Bible Hermeneutics. Retrieved from https://hermeneutics.stackexchange.com/questions/31348/two-words-for-love-in-john-2115-17 on February 5, 2024.
5. Bible Hub. Strong's Concordance. Retrieved from https://biblehub.com/lexicon/john/21-16.htm on February 5, 2024.
6. Bible Hub. Strong's Concordance. Retrieved from https://biblehub.com/lexicon/john/21-17.htm on February 5, 2024.
7. Read John 21:1-17 for the full account of this story.
8. John 21:18, TPT.
9. See John 21:19.
10. Peter is the author of 1 Peter and 2 Peter in the Bible.
11. 1 Peter 4:12-13, NKJV.
12. John 9:1-3, TPT.
13. John 9:3, AMP.
14. Read John 9:1-34 for the full account of this story.

C H A P T E R 10

WHAT ARE YOU BOWING TO?

"In this yoke lies their true freedom;
they are taller when they bow."

C.S. LEWIS, THE FOUR LOVES

In Marvel's first Avengers movie, Loki, the snarky alien villain, demanded a crowd of people on Earth bow to him and said, "... You were made to be ruled; in the end, you will always kneel."

Now more than ever, we don't want to admit how anything, or anyone, has control over us. We think we choose what has power over us and what we allow to govern our lives. The truth of God's absolute power includes a choice we all have to make—the choice of how we direct our free will. With it, will we choose to turn toward or away from God? We will **all** bow to *something;* the question is what—or maybe better stated, to whom?

Jesus knew Peter would undergo a transformation of character when he experienced the reality of denying being one of His followers. Somewhere between Peter's act of denial and the "Peter, do you love Me?" conversation he had with Jesus on the beach, Peter decided who he would bow down to.

What choice have you made?

Anything which demands our allegiance has the capacity to become an idol in our lives. God has blessed us with a lot to care for and care about. God didn't say we can't have things, good relationships, and entertainment. We just can't love them more than we love God. Anything we place our affection on above God becomes idolatry and ultimately shows us what we are bowing down to in our own hearts.

———————✥———————

What is the matter with me? the warrior thought. She pondered how could she have been so self-absorbed to think about herself during a time of crisis in one of her friends' lives. *What does it really matter what anyone else thinks about my influence on others?* she told herself. But if she really was as good as she thought she was, and as good as she felt others perceived her, why did this terrible thing happen to someone she worked with?

Well, it's on her, she justified. *I showed her how to live and conduct her life—I warned her and warned her ...* the warrior hurled a rock into the stream, punctuating her frustration.

But ... what if she doesn't make it? What if this really takes her out for good?

Memories of her friend flooded into her mind, though it had been some time since the incident had happened. *Why is this all coming back to me now?* she wondered. *Why am I thinking about her so much?* The King had taken the warrior aside when her friend fell. He knew the depth of her friend's suffering, and with immense compassion, He had shown the warrior it was time for her friend's relocation. Before He took her, the King told the warrior He was going to because He enlisted the warrior to help comfort those who would not understand the loss. She was to be a tangible representative and ambassador to those who didn't believe in the King or know He was good.

So, why now were the issues of her heart from years past stirring up? Tears filled the warrior's eyes, and she had to stop, hold onto a nearby tree, and allow herself to breathe. Even when she focused on herself, the King had chosen her to bring comfort and truth to others. *Why?* She wondered. He knows all things— even the things she could hide from others, things she even attempted to hide from herself, yet He chose her to shine His love and truth to others when they couldn't see His goodness ... even if ... even *when* ... she wasn't "good."

<hr />

EGYPT ATTITUDES

If we aren't careful, we repeat behaviors we've seen and carry on attitudes even after our circumstances change. Egypt stayed in the hearts of the Israelites after God rescued them from slavery in Egypt.

We see this time and again in the choices Israel made. When Moses went to the mountain to meet with the Lord and had been gone for longer than the newly-rescued Israelites liked, they pressured his brother, Aaron, to make them a golden calf to worship. With God on the mountain in view of their camp, they chose to worship an idol of their own making as they had seen the Egyptians do during their generations in captivity. Their firsthand experiences watching the incredible display of God's power, from the plagues in Egypt to the parting of the Red Sea as they escaped to freedom, weren't enough to change how they handled life when they couldn't understand what was happening or when things weren't going the way they expected.

Even Moses' siblings were subject to the aftereffects of having lived in Egypt. His brother, Aaron, and sister, Miriam, judged Moses for marrying a Cushite woman. While in captivity, the Israelites complained against their harsh taskmasters in Egypt, and rightfully so. Aaron and Miriam took the same attitude of complaining against leadership to grumble against Moses, their new leader, about something that was none of their business, and it cost them. The Lord Himself brought correction to Miriam and Aaron. Miriam's consequence manifested as a temporary affliction—leprosy—and she had to be removed from the camp for seven days. The entire camp of the exiled Israelites couldn't travel further until her seven days were completed.

It took a long time for God's people to recognize His character, and some never did. They had choices to make in how they perceived God, just like we still do today. The ones who started to step away from the old mindsets eventually became the leaders who took those who had endured the lessons in the desert into the Promised Land after Moses died. We have to be careful not to judge God based on our experiences with people, clergy, or even the church. God is who He declares to be in His Word, and we can't bring God down to the confines of our experience. His love for all mankind isn't based upon us; it's based upon who He is. His love remains the same whether we believe it or not.

The choice to believe remains ours.

MY MESSY LOVE VS. GOD'S LOVE

My love is flawed and imperfect. My love is messy and volatile. My love for others is both self-serving and sacrificial. I don't always have the right words to express my love, and sometimes, when I speak, all the wrong words come out. I would take a bullet for those I love and put myself in harm's way in an effort to protect them. I take on burdens I don't need to, I take things far too personally because of my flawed filters, and I can't always hear what my loved ones are saying because my love knows better for them than they do for themselves. My love is legalistic and dogmatic. My love is moody and temperamental. My love is creative and extravagant.

When I read about the Apostle Paul's definition of the kind of love we are to have for one another, I find more often than not how my ability to love comes up short. Paul defines love like this:

Love is patient.

Love is kind.

Love does not envy.

Love does not boast.

Love is not proud.

Love does not dishonor others.

Love is not self-seeking.

Love is not easily angered.

Love keeps no record of wrongs.

Love does not delight in evil.

Love rejoices with the truth.

Love always protects.

Love always trusts.

Love always hopes.

Love always perseveres.

Love never fails.[1]

My love for others flows through the filter of me. Expressing myself according to Paul's definition challenges me to remove myself from the equation. When I do so, I actually feel more empowered to love—to love more people, love more deeply, and love more selflessly.

To love in the way that Paul instructs us can take place only when we consider others first. Even something simple like being kind and accepting, rather than trying to force others to conform to our ways, creates space for more fulfilling relationships. When we make our relationships about filling our emptiness, we will find our means of loving others draining and unfulfilling. When we love others the way Paul shares, we become emptied of ourselves as we co-labor with God, who created love in the first place. When I am no longer full of myself, I become an empty vessel available to be used by God to bring blessing and provision into the lives of others. In doing so, I become more fulfilled.

ACTS OF KINDNESS

Think about acts of kindness we do when we hear of tragedy. In our desperation to connect with the situation, we look for ways to give selflessly. At the time of the writing of this book, the world watched on as twenty-four-year-old NFL Buffalo Bills player Damar Hamlin suffered a cardiac arrest on January 2, 2023, during a game against the Cincinnati Bengals. In response to this awful tragedy, Damar's GoFundMe, which he had set up two years prior with a goal of raising $2,500 towards toys for needy kids, exploded. Approximately $5.5 million was donated in the 24 hours following his collapse.[2] One month after the tragedy, more than $9 million had been raised.[3]

Why? Because people—strangers, fans, and fellow NFL players all gave out of their love and concern for Damar, and to see his genuine goal to give back to his community and always remember where he came from.

The response offered a glimpse of a way we need to love—selflessly. We thank God for Damar Hamlin's miraculous recovery and can't wait to see what the future holds for this young man.

When we use Paul's approach to loving others in the daily things we do, our lives and those around us change for the good. We work hard for those who are closest to us, and we often do so begrudgingly. We know we base our intentions on our love for them. Paul instructs us in ways we can connect our intentions with our actions towards those around us. As we go through the motions of life, going to work, making dinner, and running our homes, may we do so by love.

SUFFERING AND CRAZY LOVE

The Bible tells us of the tremendous suffering Jesus endured by being beaten, whipped, mocked, spat upon, and forced to carry His own cross to the place of His crucifixion. Jesus' suffering culminated as He hung on the cross, on our behalf, mine and yours, and for all mankind, because He loves us.[4] Jesus suffered as man, setting aside His deity.[5] Jesus set the example of how love isn't supposed to be about us, but about others. He did so in His death, and every moment He walked the Earth. He was a King who didn't come to be served, but to serve.[6]

Sounds crazy, right? But people do crazy things for love, from the dramatic deaths in *Romeo & Juliet* to sacrifice in *Titanic*. Many a best-selling book and a plethora of romantic movies recount some of the crazy things we do for love.

Growing up, my mom's number-one hobby was shopping, so this worked to my benefit as a kid during Christmas. In 1983, Cabbage Patch Dolls came out hot on the retail scene. My mother tried her hardest to get her hands on at least one in a store and never found one. Then, one day, shortly before Christmas, a friend told her of someone who was selling some authentic Cabbage Patch dolls down a back alley. Off she went! By herself! Dolls on the black market! She proudly brought home two authentic Cabbage Patch dolls for me to open on Christmas. Her love for me made the way.

How many crazy things can you think of that you have either given or been the recipient of, all in the name of love? God's love for you and me made the way for us to spend eternity with Him and for Him to assist us in the way of our journey on Earth. Since He sent His only son, Jesus, to die in our place, shouldn't we be willing to prioritize Him?

We can eat junk food or healthy foods and still live. However, our food choices aid our quality of life. Choosing God first is similar. Putting Him first brings us grace to navigate through life's hardships and enjoy the things we have and the people around us more. When we run to Him before running to our idols, He meets us. He lightens the load. He makes the impossible we are walking through bearable, even if it's moment by moment.

Scripture shows us multiple instances in which Peter, who was not only hot-tempered but also thought of himself a bit more highly than the other disciples, still followed Jesus with the others and ministered miracles and healings under Jesus' authority. His character conversion happened over time. Over breaking bread with Jesus again and again. Over traveling with Jesus. Over Jesus' grace and long-suffering with his personality.

Jesus treats us the same. The unchanging love of God remains fixed, regardless of us. We often run to and from God's love, unaware of how the very things we are craving in life come directly from Him. Even when we treat the love of God like an unbalanced scale, He remains steady and fixed, loving us as we are and where we are, which changes us.

WE OFTEN RUN TO AND FROM GOD'S LOVE, UNAWARE OF HOW THE VERY THINGS WE ARE CRAVING IN LIFE COME DIRECTLY FROM HIM.

Handing someone a set of rules to follow as a Christian doesn't work. Our God desires a relationship with us. We started our discussion on love in the last chapter with Peter's outspoken love for Christ, depicted in his arrogant declaration of how he would *never* deny Christ like the others. We then witnessed his transformation with a humble admonition of possessing brotherly love. Jesus loved Peter by having a relationship with him despite his obvious shortcomings. Jesus didn't wait until Peter had matured to accept and love him; Jesus loved Peter from day one. Peter didn't notice that when he finally stopped thinking of himself first, he acquired agape love—self-sacrificial love, 1 Corinthians 13 kind of love. This agape love Peter developed for others is a love we still glean from today, centuries later, with the scriptures and the example he left.

May we be encouraged to approach Jesus again and again, no matter how many times we fail or betray Him. His love remains fixed and true. His love defines our purpose. When we exercise agape love, the more God can use our love to change the world in which we live.

The warrior's breathing calmed. She let go of the tree and stood up straight. Her thoughts settled, and she remembered the journey she was currently on. When she lay on the battlefield, overcome with defeat and anxiety plagued her soul, she didn't know if she'd make it through her next breath. Other warriors had surrounded her with their shields connected together to keep her from the harm of the enemy raging on the battlefield, some strangers she'd never met, some she'd only known enough to recognize. They didn't come to her aid because she had never done anything for them. The King sent them. They came because their love for Him required them to extend that love to her.

She thought back to when the King held out His hand, inviting her to come on this journey—a journey which her suffering had opened before her. Terrain she would never have chosen for herself, the terrain where her greatest fears and self-love took center stage as the strongest of enemies she'd ever faced. Her good works to gain right standing meant nothing here.

In this moment, where her past converged with her future, she saw the good standing she'd always had with the King; a place to sit at His table came to her long ago as an invitation of His love—long before she had done anything for Him at all. Whether she had failed or succeeded as a leader in His realm never altered her access or standing with the King.

For her entire life, she had tried to earn her place and her position in the kingdom. She had tried to prove she was worthy of love and goodness. She *was* worthy, but she was also *not* worthy. Her worth and her value didn't come from any achievement of her own, but because of who she belonged to. She was worthy because He was worthy, and she belonged completely to Him.

There in the woods, in a small clearing where a flat rock was warmed by the sun, the warrior pulled her sword from its sheath and knelt, holding it high with extended hands. She bowed her head and said, "My King, how I love You. My heart is Yours alone. Thank You for choosing me. Thank You for loving me. With all my being, I will love and serve You ..."

As she spoke these words, a powerful wind swirled around her, lifting the strands of her hair and causing the leaves to dance and swirl about her. She opened her eyes to see what was causing the gust, and *there He was!* Her King stood before her in splendor and glory, His eyes sparkling, His smile brighter than the sun. "Come to Me, daughter!" He laughed and opened His arms to her as if calling a small child. With no formality or ceremony, the warrior dropped her sword and ran into His arms.

ENDNOTES

1. See 1 Corinthians 13:4-8, NIV.
2. Reynolds, Tim (January 3, 2023) *Fans Give Millions to Damar Hamlin's Toy Drive for Kids.* AP News. https://apnews.com/article/damar-hamlin-fundrais-er-toy-drive-gofundme-bills-cd61ceed517af7c53637ba23644801c9 accessed on January 16, 2023.
3. *Damar Hamlin GoFundMe Page Raises More Than $9 Million* (February 12, 2023). Philanthropy News Digest. https://philanthropynewsdigest.org/news/damar-hamlin-gofundme-page-raises-more-than-9-millionaccessed on February 7, 2024.
4. See Matthew 27:27-44 for the biblical account.
5. See Philippians 2:7.
6. See Matthew 20:28.

CHAPTER 11

WHAT, THEN, IF—

*"To defeat the darkness out there,
you must defeat the darkness inside yourself."*

THE OPPRESSOR TO LUCY
The Chronicles of Narnia: The Voyage of the Dawn Treader

As she stepped back from their embrace, she began to notice how everything around her looked familiar ... but different. With no sense of how much time had passed, she was amazed at all she had discovered about herself, especially her ideology. Reflection on and rediscovering situations in her life gave her a different perspective, creating a new sense of energy. The old thoughts and memories didn't weigh her down like they once did. Alone in her thoughts, she continued to ponder the feeling that she had found pieces to a puzzle she didn't even know had been missing. Her King stopped her and spoke as if He knew what she'd been thinking about. "I've set before you two doors; they are doors of the past and the present that now must converge together to make the future. You don't have to deny what you have been through. The pain, the mistakes, and the losses are all part of what makes you uniquely you. You don't need to try and keep them separate."

He sat among large rocks and called her over to sit across from Him so they were face to face, and He continued, "You needed to look back so you can now look forward with faith and expectation that I will move on your behalf. I will move this very mountain if it gets in the way of the plan I have for you. I have plans to prosper you and not to cause you any harm. You can't go back to the past; you can only learn from it. I promise you I am not done with this part of your story yet. Take Me by the hand and find your new grace for today. Even if at times it seems the whole world is against you, remember I am always for you and with you."

At 11 years old, I watched my mom pace in and out of her walk-in closet while shaking both her hands frantically, as if something sticky was on them and she was trying to get it off. She kept repeating the same name over and over, sometimes in a whisper and then loudly in great anguish. I remember watching and waiting, wanting to know and not wanting to know all at the same time. I've tried so many times to block out what she told me. I don't remember the drive to my aunt and uncle's house, but I remember walking in the back door like I had many times before. It was August 6, 1983. The house was full of people, but the only sound to be heard was my 13-year-old cousin Mark's lament, even from the back of the house. His identical twin brother Louis, precious Louis, died in a 4-wheeler accident at a friend's camp.

My five cousins were the closest thing I had to brothers. We went to school together, and since my mom was a single parent, I spent a lot of time at their house after school. As the only girl, I was usually observing the twins and their older brother's stunts while the two youngest played nearby. They had fun in everything they did, from jumping off the garage roof into a pile of old tires to using mattresses to surf down the stairs in the house. Together we enjoyed making forts in the far away unfinished parts of the attic with hanging strands of beads left over from the '70s as our doorway. I lacked their fearlessness, but I enjoyed the company and entertainment nonetheless.

Mark and Louis were as twins as twins could be. Charming to all and welcoming to having you on their side. Mark rooted for the Cowboys, Louis, the Dolphins. Mark listened to Led Zeplin and Lynard Skynyrd. Louis listened to Rush. Both loved big, laughed hard, and made all the girls blush. They enjoyed switching roles, wearing each other's clothes, attending each other's classes, and dating each other's girls.

And now Louis was gone.

Even after his passing, I kept observing.

I noticed Aunt Maryann, who was new to her faith in Jesus, when her son Louis passed. Rather than blame God, she chose to cling to Him instead. She endured the darkness of the great loss with the light of her faith in Jesus Christ. She attended church services and Bible studies, read her Bible, and prayed. She had friends who shared her faith rally around her to help her learn and grow her faith as the glue to hold her husband and the remaining four boys together through the intensity of grief.

When I became a little older, I started going home alone after school. I'd have a list of chores to complete before my mom came home from work and time to be left alone with my thoughts. I'd spend it listening to music and often crying, questioning why God didn't take me instead of Louis. I questioned why someone so beloved by his family and the community could die. I told myself no one would have missed me as much. A remedy, I felt, could take the pain away from those I loved and couldn't handle watching suffer, especially his surviving twin, Mark. Mark and I remained close while we were in high school, and being family, we'd talk of memories with Louis, but not how we felt. No one talked about how they felt. We all lived with the loss but couldn't put words towards the emptiness. Grief often isolates those affected. I didn't understand then how my aunt's faith kept her family connected.

Years passed, and my tears subsided, but the question I asked of God through my eleven-year-old broken heart of *why not me instead* remained buried until I was finally able to recognize it as an adult. As a young mom with identical twins within my triplets, my perspective changed. Having my own children enabled me to understand what I began to see a long time ago, yet couldn't articulate. It was never my responsibility to take away the pain of others around me, but an opportunity for Jesus to.

When we call out to Jesus in the midst of the storms of life, He doesn't just calm the storm to address the initial crisis at hand; He equips us for a greater purpose.

THE STORM OF FAITH

Remember when we talked about the question Jesus asked the disciples when He calmed the storm in the boat in chapter two? These were the same questions He left me with when I invited Him to calm the storm of anxiety after my second eye surgery. All three accounts of the story of Jesus calming the storm have slight variations about Jesus questioning the disciples about their faith.

"Why are you so fearful? How is it you have no faith?"[1]

"Why are you fearful, O you of little faith?"[2]

"Where is your faith?"[3]

In one account, Jesus asked them before He calmed the storm, and in the other two, he asked afterward. The accounts also all vary slightly on what Jesus said, which happens in normal storytelling based on each person's perspective and memory. However, Matthew, Mark, and Luke all continue their Gospels with the same story following the account of the storm. The boat landed where the demoniac lived among the tombs. Here, those present with Jesus would witness the deliverance and restoration of a man everyone had left to his torment by himself. Here, the disciples needed their faith.

Could the question Jesus asked them about their faith when He calmed the storm have been more about what they were going to encounter than the storm that provoked the question in the first place? After I invited Jesus to calm the storm of my anxiety, the question of my faith incited the journey to uncover my seed of faith. Faith I would need for multiple surgeries, dealing with the outcome of two failed cornea transplants, and learning to adjust to life with not only a different appearance, but also a loss of vision.

Jesus didn't ask the question to make the disciples feel bad or stupid; He asked because He knew what was coming next. Jesus knew His disciples would need their faith for what they were about to witness and for what He had called them to do, especially when He could no longer be with them.

WHAT, THEN, IF—

What, then, if—

what I am believing for hasn't happened yet?

What, then, if—

what I believed for doesn't happen?

What, then, if—

the casket goes into the ground,

and the promise of life is now behind us?

What, then, if—

> *the divorce becomes final,*

> *and we have to start over and rebuild our lives?*

What, then, if—

> *the diagnosis is confirmed,*

> *and there isn't anything else the doctors can do?*

Life leaves us pretty beat up at times. Crisis and trauma know no limits. Regardless of our age, race, size, or political party, we will all come face to face with hard times.

"What then shall we say to these things? If God *is* for us, who *can be* against us?"[4]

CHOOSE WHOSE VOICE YOU WILL LISTEN TO

I forgot my phone. I usually take a few moments of solitude behind closed doors when I get ready for my day to listen to a teaching or music or sneak in a phone call without having listening ears. My sacred place. Oddly enough, with my door ajar, I couldn't help but notice a plethora of sounds from various locations in my house.

The living room became the homeschool classroom for my youngest son, with instruction flowing through the television. Meanwhile, my four college students usually juggled their online, hybrid schedules of synchronous and asynchronous classes with their earbuds on. (You can guess which year it is!)

However, no one had their earbuds in on this day. I stood in my doorway, hearing multiple teachings coming from different rooms. I found it impossible to focus on one voice. Just when I seemed to be hearing one lesson, voices from the other rooms crowded it out. If I wanted to focus in on one of the voices being streamed, I would have to figure out a way to shut out all the other voices and draw closer to the one I desired to hear.

You and I need to do the same thing each and every day to hear the voice of God. We often don't hear God because we treat His voice like all the others swirling around in our minds, picking and choosing what we agree with or what we have the time and space for.

Chances are you have areas of your life you live intentionally about. Maybe you focus on a certain eating and exercise plan and work to stay within those parameters. Maybe you are diligent about your investments, spend time researching the market trends, and adjust your investment portfolio accordingly. To live intentionally as a believer in Jesus Christ involves practicing certain habits. If we aren't careful, these habits can become a catalog of religious duties we check off our to-do list without ever reaping the benefits God intended. God created us for a relationship with Him accessed through our faith by His grace. We are responsible for the way we approach this relationship.

The circumstances we deal with in life don't always leave us feeling like God is for us. If anything, we can feel like God is against us when our lives are plagued with trial and heartache.

We must choose not to live by the roller coaster of emotions and feelings life generates. We have an awesome privilege to live by faith. Faith enables us to see what we can't with our natural eyes. To live by faith opens us up to live through the hard things in life with eternal promises to strengthen us for the days ahead.

How, then, do I live by faith when I suffer, face trials, and find myself in crisis?

TO LIVE BY FAITH OPENS US UP TO LIVE THROUGH THE HARD THINGS IN LIFE WITH ETERNAL PROMISES TO STRENGTHEN US FOR THE DAYS AHEAD.

THE ARMOR OF GOD

Early in my Christian walk, I was taught to pray and *put on the armor of God* when life's circumstances were less than ideal.

Despite my diligence in praying and picturing myself putting the armor of God on, I rarely *felt* like I could stand against my own thoughts, let alone "the rulers, against the authorities, against the powers of this dark world and against the spiritual forces of evil"[5] Paul talked about. If anything, *putting on the armor of God* made me feel less than par because I wasn't able to access the attributes the pieces of armor were supposed to represent in my Christian life. I didn't understand that for the armor to be effective as Paul's writings intended, it would require yielding my heart to the Lord. To live according to "our own truth," even if some aspects of "our truth" line up with God's Word, will not protect us spiritually like the armor of God was intended to.

"Finally, be strong in the Lord and in His mighty power. Put on the full armor of God, so that you can take your stand against the devil's schemes. For our struggle is not against flesh and blood, but against the rulers, against the authorities, against the powers of this dark world and against the spiritual forces of evil in the heavenly realms.

"Therefore, put on the full armor of God, so that when the day of evil comes, you may be able to stand your ground, and after you have done everything, to stand.

Stand firm then, with the belt of truth buckled around your waist, with the breastplate of righteousness in place, and with your feet fitted with the readiness that comes from the gospel of peace. In addition to all this, take up the shield of faith, with which you can extinguish all the flaming arrows of the evil one. Take the helmet of salvation and the sword of the Spirit, which is the Word of God.

"And pray in the Spirit on all occasions with all kinds of prayers and requests. With this in mind, be alert and always keep on praying for all the Lord's people."[6]

The journey I embarked upon through my suffering authenticated my faith as a manner of living rather than a series of words to recite in an attempt to achieve an outcome of my own making.

HELMET OF SALVATION

"Do not conform to the pattern of this world, but be transformed by the renewing of your mind. Then you will be able to test and approve what God's will is—His good, pleasing, and perfect will."[7]

We must first take the question of faith and decide if we will yield our hearts to the eternal salvation Christ Jesus extends to us. Once we do, we firmly place the **helmet of salvation** upon our heads and can start the work of protecting our thoughts. In order to see our minds change and produce the abundant life Jesus died to give us,[8] we need a safe place for our thoughts to dwell. We must discover the truth of who we are in God's Word. Being aware of our thoughts and protecting them with the Word of God blocks Satan from bringing the consequences of sin into our thoughts.

We renew our minds and our thoughts by reading and meditating on the Word of God.

BELT OF TRUTH

"I will meditate on Your precepts
and think about Your ways."[9]

As we submerge ourselves in God's Word, we discover truth. We wrap ourselves with the **belt of truth** to live and govern our lives by. To do so, we not only need to understand the truth but to live as people of truth. To give our word and keep our word. To live with integrity. To know that satan is a liar and to have enough truth in us to recognize his lies for what they are. When we lie, we operate under the enemy's rules and anarchy while also giving him access to our lives. Jesus is the way, the truth, and the life.[10] The truth is in Jesus.

I encourage you to read the Bible daily and take time to meditate on the scriptures. There are many translations of the Bible available to us today, each offering variations of language that can help make the study more exciting and interesting. Whether you have an old-fashioned paper and ink favorite, you read on a Bible app, or listen to the Bible being read—just do it. Fill your mind and your spirit with God's Word and welcome the transformation that ensues.

We weren't meant to travel this journey of life ill-equipped. God gave us a travel manual, His Word, the Bible. We shouldn't just read it when we get lost; we should read it regularly to familiarize ourselves with the terrain.

BREASTPLATE OF RIGHTEOUSNESS

"But first and most importantly seek (aim at, strive after) His kingdom and His righteousness [His way of doing and being right—the attitude and character of God], and all these things will be given to you also."[11]

Our breastplate fastens to the belt of truth. The Word of God is the truth. As believers in God's Word, we choose to live according to His way of doing and being with the attitude and character of God we see in the scriptures. God's Spirit, the Holy Spirit, leads us in the ways in which we live. He not only leads us; He empowers us to live righteously. It's impossible to do so in my own strength. God's grace enables me to live righteously, just like God's grace offers me salvation. There is nothing I can do of my own strength to earn God's grace, to earn my salvation, or to earn my breastplate of righteousness or any other part of my armor. My job is to live in right standing with God. In doing so, I am protecting my heart and vital organs spiritually.

"Guard your heart above all else, for it is the source of life."[12]

Some of the choices I make to live righteously involve setting boundaries for myself. I choose to protect what I allow into my heart through my eyes and ears. I stay close to the Holy Spirit to keep my spirit safe and whole. Why would I take a boat into the water only to purposely put holes in it for the boat to sink? My armor protects my heart. Why would I toss my armor to the ground during an enemy attack?

FEET SANDALED WITH READINESS FOR THE GOSPEL OF PEACE

"How beautiful on the mountains are the feet of those who bring good news, who proclaim peace, who bring good tidings, who proclaim salvation, who say to Zion, 'Your God reigns!'"[13]

The sandals depicted in this passage are those of a Roman soldier, which had bottoms similar to the athletic cleats we see today. They were able to grip difficult terrain that other shoes couldn't—not exactly what I'd picture as shoes of *peace!* I picture more of a ballet shoe where I could twirl around with no cares in an open meadow. Okay, not really. Chances are, whatever way you picture peace isn't really what Paul is talking about. He gives us the reminder we all need to share the Gospel with others—anytime, anywhere—and be willing to reach others not easily reached with the message of salvation.

When I find moments to testify of God's goodness, my faith is strengthened along with those I reach out to. Testifying reminds us that it's not about our accomplishments in the first place. Testifying takes our focus off of the circumstances and places it on the One who can do something about our circumstances.

MY FAITH IS STRENGTHENED WHEN I TESTIFY.

SHIELD OF FAITH

"For we walk by faith, not by sight."[14]

Oh, how I have come to understand what it means to walk by faith and not by sight. The weapons I wield are, in one hand, the Word of God—my sword—and, in the other, my shield of faith. I now understand what Paul meant when he said, "The weapons of our warfare are not carnal, but mighty through God to the pulling down of strongholds."[15] Neither of these weapons is about my skills or my strengths. They are about what I believe (strongholds) and how I direct my faith. I believe in He who sent me; I believe in all He has provided for me. I receive all He has given to me. What do you believe?

My prayer is for my name and your name to be written alongside the heroes of faith in Hebrews 11. By faith ... Laurie believed God ... By faith _____(fill in your name) believed God _____(and what's in your heart to believe God for).

SWORD OF THE SPIRIT

"For the Word of God is alive and active. Sharper than any double-edged sword, it penetrates even to the dividing soul and spirit, joints and marrow; it judges the thoughts and attitudes of the heart."[16]

The Sword of the Spirit is God's Word accompanied by the Holy Spirit. We are to defend ourselves by speaking God's Word against anything that is contrary to God's promises in the Bible.

Jesus showed us how to use the Sword of the Spirit after being led by the Holy Spirit into the wilderness to fast and pray for forty days and then be tempted by Satan. Jesus responded to Satan all three times by first saying, "It is written," and then quoting the Word of God.[17] We, too, when Satan comes at us, can say, "It is written ..."

For example, when I am struggling with thoughts about fear, I remember what is written: "So do not fear, for I am with you; do not be dismayed, for I am your God. I will strengthen you and help you; I will uphold you with my righteous right hand."[18] As a matter of fact, the Bible has 365 scriptures reminding us to "Fear Not." Seems like God knew fear would be a daily issue for some of us, and we can replace our fearful thoughts with scripture. That is how we wield the Sword of the Spirit.

When we speak the Word of God, we are telling our thoughts what to think and the very atmosphere around us to come into alignment with it.

I *put on the armor of God* so I can be strong in the Lord and His mighty power. I put on the armor of God so I can stand—firm— against the devil's schemes. Now I know that the action of putting this armor on is through my daily choices to live intentionally.

I learned to pray by imitating what I observed while attending my first Christian church in the '90s. I'm so thankful for a Bible-believing church that took prayer and God seriously. I discovered how to pray in the Spirit and to pray God's Word back to Him. I didn't understand the value of what I was learning to implement in my own life, but by praying in accordance with scripture, I am able to align my thoughts with God's ways. For example, the Bible tells us to pray for our enemies. This is not something I am naturally inclined to do out of my own volition. Prayers that are contrary to God's Word have zero effect, so having God's Word to navigate through my time of petitioning helps me to keep my opinion of what God needs to do to a minimum and is a great guide for me to this day.

Throughout the years, I have cultivated my prayer life and studied prayer modeled in the Bible. I've read books on prayer, attended prayer meetings, hosted small groups on prayer, and have been diligent in setting time aside for prayer. None of this qualifies me, but more realistically, it quantifies the inadequacy I feel on the topic of prayer. The more I learn, the more I realize how much I do not know. All I can do is share openly about where I come up short. God remains faithful—especially to His Word. I have endured seasons where my prayer life consisted of car prayers and shower petitions before the Lord. I've spent many nights whispering only the word *"help"* through tears during difficult seasons. I have fallen asleep during my scheduled prayer time and most certainly battled distraction through every season life brings. I recently looked back on an old prayer journal and saw how I had treated prayer like giving God my "Honey-do" list—my list of "change these things" and "change these people" to make my life easier.

I have concluded there isn't a formula to prayer, but there are certain attributes of prayer we can glean from. First and foremost, don't feel like you have to have it all figured out. God knew we wouldn't always know what to pray for, so He provided help. "Likewise the Spirit also helps in our weaknesses. For we do not know what we should pray for as we ought, but the Spirit Himself makes intercession for us with groanings which cannot be uttered."[19]

Prayer is the place where we learn to commune with God. We most certainly can offer our petitions and requests, but we must also learn to take time and make space to be still, to quiet ourselves. This may feel awkward at first. Try starting with a minute and then add another as you get used to it. When your mind wanders off, just go back and get it.[20] Being still is a discipline we practice. When we do, we learn to hear in the stillness, His voice. His voice to direct us in life, comfort us in hardship, challenge us to follow His ways, and change us into His likeness. As you learn to cultivate these disciplines, you will find you'll start to crave this time. Prayer becomes the intentional place where we develop a relationship with God and see our faith grow.

> GOD'S VOICE DIRECTS US, COMFORTS US, CHALLENGES US TO FOLLOW HIS WAYS AND CHANGE INTO HIS LIKENESS.

Prayer is where we take God at His Word, quote His Word back to Him, and discover how to contend against the enemy of our souls. We emerge from prayer with our armor on and our shield of faith raised, ready to quench the fiery darts of the enemy— and we stand.

WHEN OPPOSITION COMES

With my thoughts and vital organs protected and my life governed by truth, I am ready to share the Gospel of peace. My faith protects me from what the enemy throws at me, and I declare the Word of God has the final say over my life and my circumstances.

Therefore, I stand against the old mindsets and lies that try to make me question my worth, my relationships, and God's goodness towards me. I stand against bad news and loss for myself, my family, and my loved ones. When the lies appear to line up with circumstances happening around me, I stand, fully armored against the "rulers, authorities, the powers of this dark world and the spiritual forces of evil."[21]

What, then, if—

I get tired while I stand against

the wicked schemes of the enemy?

Sometimes, our faith walk feels like we are on a diet we keep hearing about from friends, and everyone else is getting results except us. You are following all the plans, measuring your food, and you never cheat. You are drinking your water and exercising before and after work, but instead of losing weight, you managed to gain a few pounds. You wonder why and just want to quit. But then you get around a group of people who have struggled like you have and encourage you to keep going even when it's hard, even when you don't see results, even when it would seem easier to quit.

Armed with this encouragement, you stay the course, overcome the plateau, and finally begin to see results.

Fellowship with other people of faith gives us the tools we need to walk out our faith. Not only can we encourage, challenge, and pray for one another, but we can also let others see themselves through our eyes.

ARE WE WILLING TO ACCEPT OUR SCARS?

"This is how it will be. Accept it and get on with life," was my surgeon's response after the second cornea transplant didn't improve my vision as either of us had hoped. *Accept it?* There was a part of me that felt I needed to refuse his words if I were to continue to stand in faith. *Accept it?* One of my friends who knew I was struggling to be around people said to me one day, "Laurie, I don't even see what's happened with your eye when I look at you; I see the friend I love."

I wanted to cover my eye and hide what I had been through from even myself. If we aren't careful, we can try to cover up our scars instead of seeing the beauty in them.

I love the part in Pixar's *Cars 2* movie where Mater is being prepared to go undercover to help solve the malicious series of accidents during the World Cup his best friend Lightning McQueen was racing in. Despite Mater's numerous attempts to communicate he isn't really a spy, he finds himself engulfed in this new endeavor. When he is approached to have his dents buffed out to prepare for his disguise, he refuses. He wants to keep his dents because they represent memories made with Lightning McQueen. At this moment, he and Lightning weren't even talking to each other after a misunderstanding that cost McQueen first place in the first race of the competition. A misunderstanding Mater wasn't willing to let change his sentiment toward his friend or the memories they shared together. He *accepted* his dents and found meaning in them.

Unknown to her, my friend's words gave me permission to *accept it.*

My faith didn't have to change. I didn't need to deny the outcome. I can accept my current set of circumstances while walking in faith. It is my job to know what I believe.

ARE WE WILLING TO WAIT?

One of my adult daughters, who had the undiagnosed bleeding disorder as a teen, said to me in between my surgeries, "Mom, every time I received prayer, I thought, *'This is it, I am healed.'* And I wasn't yet; it's a process."

Years ago, while my daughters were hospitalized and undergoing testing, friends and family would share the story we find in scripture of the woman Jesus healed with the issue of blood.[22] Every time someone sent me the scripture references or prayed them over my daughters, I clung to the part of the story where Jesus healed. However, I kept skipping over how long she had been afflicted. I disregarded her waiting—twelve years of waiting—and how she spent all she had on doctors and treatments. Every time she paid a bill and attempted treatment, she hoped her situation would change. She exercised her faith every time she tried something new.

Again and again, what she tried did not work.

Maybe your need for healing isn't something you are dealing with in your body, but in the way your mind thinks. Maybe you battle addictions that plague your thoughts, and you've tried and tried in your own strength to walk away and have a fresh start. You tell yourself it shouldn't be this hard. Don't give up on whatever you need help with. Whether it's a miracle in your body or freedom in your mind, don't give up, and don't stop doing those things you know bring freedom. Keep crying out to God in prayer and declaring God's Word over your life and the circumstances you face. Thank God ahead of time for the manifestation of what you seek to happen in your life, even before you see it.

Whether we are learning to live with our scars, waiting for our miracles, or some combination of both, we have a choice in how we will live. More than ever, we can recognize we are living in a war. We struggle, and battles rage around us. And just when we think things can't get any more complicated, they do. How, then, are we to stand for our mental health and for our families when we ourselves feel uncertain as times unfold around us?

By praying, reading our Bibles, and having church fellowship, we feed ourselves spiritually.

We find our identity and purpose in God's love. He loves us perfectly despite our failures and weaknesses, and like Peter, His love changes us.

Faith isn't just about believing for miracles to happen in our lives; faith is about aligning ourselves for miracles to happen. In order to believe, you must lose a part of yourself. You lose the part of yourself that wants to understand. The part of yourself that likes to keep score. In order to gain life, we must first lose it. We can hold on to our preconceived ideas and opinions, our need to figure out and understand, or we can let it all go—like Elsa's been telling us to for years.

> IN ORDER TO BELIEVE, YOU MUST LOSE THE PART OF YOURSELF THAT WANTS TO UNDERSTAND.

WHAT, THEN, IF—

What, then, if—

God never heals my eye the way I know He can?

For me, the story is simple. I worship Him, love Him, and serve Him like He has already restored my vision.

Because that is faith.

When we get our eyes off of our circumstances and onto God and remember His nature, our vision changes; when we see God extend grace to us like the father to the prodigal son; when we come to know Jesus who loves instead of punishes, we can handle anything that comes our way.

GRACE LIKE MANNA

We need different amounts of grace through different seasons of our lives. We don't have access to grace without Jesus, and we need to establish and affirm Jesus daily as Lord in our lives.

There isn't a daily limit to the grace we have access to. We don't reach a certain amount and then hear God say, "Come back tomorrow."

I need grace every day. Grace becomes my superpower to endure the circumstances of my life. Grace helps us through the hard things. And like manna, we can have all we want each and every day. Also, like manna, we can't store up grace for tomorrow. We have to trust God for a fresh supply every day and know that we have access to all we need through the differing circumstances life brings. My prayer for you is to cease from striving. As you cease from striving, may you see the gift of grace that has always been available to you, and may you receive the grace you need to endure life and the trials that come your way.

Just like I can't trust every thought that comes to my mind or every emotion of my heart, I can't trust in using my works to attain what God already gave me. That's like taking the birthday gift you received and going back to the store to try and pay for it again. Remember grace is a:

G – Gift from God

R – Received by faith

A – Available every day

C – Ceased from trying to earn by works

E – Encountered in every situation

THE FINAL WORD

If you could see yourself through my eyes, you wouldn't see any imperfections. You would see a warrior on a winning team sent to wage war. You would see strength and honor. You would see scars from battles well fought and the courage to get up and try again. You would see faith refined by fire, hope redirected, and love encompassing everything pertaining to you and the life you have, which is worth living. You would see, despite the loss, you have gained character which couldn't be attained another way. You would also hear me reminding you that you were created for such a time as this.

~~~~~~~~~

There was a great sense of a newness of life. Gone were the days of death and defeat. The once stagnant air was now sweet with the fragrance of spring in full blossom, and a lush green carpet filled the landscape everywhere the eyes could see. Birds were singing and dancing about as if weightless in the air. One couldn't help but breathe in deeply, hoping this moment would never end.

I bowed on one knee before my King.

With my armor clad securely about me, I bowed my head. The King gently pulled my chin up to lock my gaze upon His. This moment of His admiration upon me became forever etched into my heart and mind. Never did I foresee how my service offered great value to the one I served.

Without unlocking His gaze, the great King raised His mighty sword to touch my right shoulder and gently swooped it over my head to my left shoulder. K N I G H T E D.

"Rise," He commanded. "Arise, My warrior, and stand."

In this moment, I knew now more than ever that I could no longer be pulled into the darkness and remain trapped. I no longer had to pretend to be someone I was not. Gone were the days of the torment, of being double-minded, of second-guessing my decisions.

With firm confidence, I stood with assurance, knowing who I was and what I was created for. Despite my years of service to my King, I had too often served from my own reservoir of strength and faced my limitations like a block in a maze. It wasn't until I lost my sight that I could finally find my way out. I can see more clearly now because I had to lose my sight to see what I believe.

WHAT WILL WE DO?

My future battles are far from over. But this war I fight in is no longer the war of being trapped within the darkness of my mind. The only war I must engage in now belongs to my King. The ultimate battle is as old as time, between good and evil. A battle for fellow warriors to find their place in this vast army.

There are many souls at stake. Souls who have no voice for themselves—the oppressed, the widowed, the orphans, and the unborn. Those trapped in slavery. The cry of the innocence of their blood reaches our King with every breath we take.

What will we do? Will we remain silent, hoping no one notices what we really stand for in a time of great opposition? Or will we stand ready for battle?

The enemy isn't the one to be feared. We must fear our apathy and unwillingness to yield to the ways of our King. Our ignorant stupor plays into the hands of the enemy as we are dumbed down and weakened into believing our voice means nothing.

Our King spoke our very existence into being and has shown us the power of unity and the spoken word, especially when it's His Word coming forth from our lips. What will we say? What will we align ourselves with?

The strategies for victory are ours for the taking. We don't have to come up with our own strength, for our King even provides us with that.

I ask you, my fellow sojourners, will you take His hand and allow Him to help you see through the darkness?

ENDNOTES

1. See Mark 4:35-41 NKJV.
2. See Matthew 8:23-27, NKJV.
3. See Luke 8:22-25, NKJV.
4. Romans 8:31, NKJV.
5. Ephesians 6:12, NIV.
6. Ephesians 6:10-18, NIV, emphasis added.
7. Romans 12:2, NIV.
8. See John 10:10.
9. Psalm 119:15, HCSB.
10. See John 14:6.
11. Matthew 6:33, AMP.
12. Proverbs 4:23, HCSB.
13. Isaiah 52:7, NIV.
14. 2 Corinthians 5:7, ESV.
15. 2 Corinthians 10:4, KJV.
16. Hebrews 4:12, NIV.
17. Read Matthew 4:1-11 for the account.
18. Isaiah 41:10, NIV.
19. Romans 8:26, NKJV.
20. Graham Cook says God told him, "When your mind wanders off, just go back and get it."
21. Ephesians 6:12, NIV.
22. Read Matthew 9:20-22 for the account.

E P I LOGUE

*"The lies we hear are gentle whispers that have spoken
to us for so long. We adopt them as our own,
and we make an agreement with them every time
we speak them out of our mouths."*

LAURIE DEVERNOE

I shared how my husband managed my intense eye drop and medication schedule going around the clock. He and one of our daughters set alarms, adjusted their work schedules, and slept on the couch neighboring the one I rested on. They kept a log of the drops and medications they administered to me and monitored my temperature to report even the slightest increase. The seriousness of the infection looming so close to my brain scared everyone, including the doctors. Each of my five children alongside my husband found their place to assist in our home and make up for what I could no longer do. They sat beside me, held my hand, and wept with me and for me.

Yet, as close as they all were to me, not one of them could decide for me how I would direct my faith. The choice was mine and mine alone. While my husband has faith more like Job, unmovable, mine...well, I had some reckoning to do.

Only I could sort through the experience of what was happening to my body and the emotional roller coaster that went along with it. I spent countless hours in my surgeons' offices. It was not uncommon for a surgeon to sit down next to me with a few instruments within reach—sometimes to remove stitches, other times to sew new ones in. If someone had told me I would endure stitches being put in or taken out of my eye while awake, I would have never believed them! Each time they ran a vision test where I needed to look at the blue dot in the machine and always had to say I couldn't see it, was demoralizing.

When my life looked like it was falling apart and spiraling into a pit of despair, I could finally see the only way to access the grace I needed was to come—anxious with the question of my faith—all over again to Jesus. And I discovered the grace He extended to me for my salvation is the same grace offered to me daily for my life.

My unbelief wasn't just centered on who I dictated God to represent in my life, but on who I viewed myself as when I looked in the mirror and the impact I was making in my little corner of the world—which consisted mostly of my living room. Grace gave me the strength to welcome God into the darkness my unbelief led me into, and grace enabled me to see truth so I could find my way out. Little did I know how the truth of God's good nature had prepared my heart to discover the faith I would need to move forward from my circumstances.

MEDICAL SUMMARY

After the first cornea transplant, a portion of my damaged cornea was sent for pathology. Throughout a series of communications between the lab and my doctor's office, there was a discussion of how the condition of my right eye may have been acquired from being on the spectrum of a rare eye condition known as Iridocorneal Endothelial Syndrome (ICE). Here, the inner layer (the endothelial) of the five layers of the cornea dysfunctions. The endothelial cells are not supposed to regenerate. With ICE, the cells start to replicate and spread, which can damage the cornea, cause glaucoma, and damage the iris.[1]

As of the writing of this book, I have had seven eye surgeries, two being cornea transplants. The first transplant was damaged from the cataract removal, and the second was rejected from an auto-immune response almost a year after the transplant. I was starting to see, though dimly, after the second transplant up until the auto-immune response. Since then, I have had little to no sight out of my right eye. Several of my doctors feel the initial infection and resulting inflammation in my eye caused damage to my optic nerve, which cannot be treated medically, regardless of how clear the cornea is.

With my iris (the colored part) also removed, there is no muscular structure to open and close—how your pupil dilates and contracts. So, even if I had a perfect, clear corneal transplant and lens implant, that important pupillary sphincter muscle – the iris, which helps control how much light and where it focuses the light on your retina, remains fully and permanently dilated. So, it would be light-sensitive, and my vision would still be blurry (like when you go for an eye exam and have your eyes dilated). It would never be sharp and clear.

I need a miracle for this eye to see again.

Currently, I live with the "rejected" cornea transplant and a mustard seed of faith. My surgeon has left it up to me if I'd like another transplant—a third transplant.

For now, I remain undecided on another transplant, knowing it wouldn't restore my vision, knowing I need a miracle to see again from my right eye—but I know a guy—His name is Jesus Christ, and He happens to be a miracle worker.

So, friends and fellow sojourners, if you see me at a church meeting and the song "Way Maker"[2] is being played, you will see me take my glasses off at the bridge of the song, cover my left eye (my seeing eye) with my left hand, and raise my right hand and right eye toward heaven as I sing along.

A dear friend recently said to me, "You are one of the people who knows that your body is the house of miracles. You know it's not the church building, but you know that the temple (of the Holy Spirit) is your body, is the house of miracles. It's a testament to your faith and your steadfastness in the Lord and understanding of relationship that you don't have to be in any specific place. You don't need somebody else to lay hands to heal you because the Lord lives inside you and can overcome you. You could wake up and be healed; you could be in the middle of a meal and be healed."

I now know from being unable to see that my healing doesn't come from anything I can do to serve God; it doesn't come from any specific person or people praying for me, but it comes from the finished work of Christ. Through each surgery, every doctor visit, every tear and pleading. Through each prayer and every moment of every day, I rest in knowing it's already been done.

My job is to "only believe."[3]

MY HEALING DOESN'T COME FROM ANYTHING I CAN DO TO SERVE GOD—IT COMES FROM THE FINISHED WORK OF CHRIST.

ENDNOTES

1. *Fact Sheet: Iridocorneal Endothelial (ICE) Syndrome.* Posted July 20, 2020 by Glaucoma Australia. https://glaucoma.org.au/sites/default/files/inline-files/Iridocorneal%20Endothelial%20Syndrome%20July%202020_0.pdf accessed on January 12, 2024.
2. "Way Maker" written by Sinach © 2016 Integrity Music Europe. CCLI# 7115744 To watch the official video: https://www.youtube.com/watch?v=n4XWfwL-HeLM.
3. See Mark 5:36.

PHOTO GALLERY

The first photo taken after the eye infection started in January 2022—it was taken to prove to loved ones I was okay

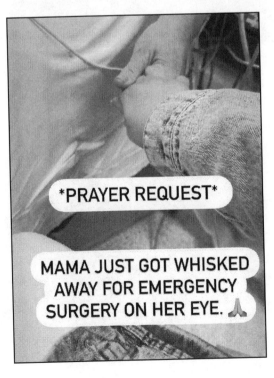

One of my kids Instagram requests for prayer for the emergency surgery on February 2, 2022

First time I left the house with makeup and an attempt at doing my hair to speak at a Mom's meeting to promote *Coffee House Parenting*—March 2022

For all my fellow Marvel Fans—my **Odin** Eye Patch a friend made for me on his 3D printer. Thanks, Joe! —March 2022

My husband and
I during my first
outdoor adventure—
April 2022

My family and I
during my first
outdoor adventure –
April 2022

My husband and I on my 50th birthday. He tried to look as cool as me with an eye patch— April 2022

None of the family looked quite as cool as I did in an eye patch —April 2022

Speaking at a Mom's Luncheon—April 2022

My first elevation hike with an eye patch—May 2022

My perfectly matching cheetah eye patch I never would have bought for myself.
Thanks Alicia!
—May 2022

This is me with Louis (left) and Mark (right), we may have just gotten caught coming our hair over—Early 1970s

Our last family photo before Rebecca left for school in Florida
—August 2022

Believing in faith for my healing at a prayer meeting
—June 2023

Laurie Devernoe is a long-time Jesus lover and coffee enthusiast. To her, they go hand in hand.

An author, dynamic speaker, ordained minister, and board-certified mental health coach, Laurie is dedicated to serving families and individuals of all backgrounds. She is passionate about helping people access their faith, strengthen their relationships, and be equipped to live impactful lives.

Laurie discovered how sharing her favorite seasonal coffee drink and her faith in Jesus with others fueled her to keep up with her children—eighteen-month-old triplet daughters and infant son. Eight years later, her second son was born.

Married to Ron for over 25 years and living in Upstate New York, Laurie draws from her decades of parenting experience and education to pour into the lives of others in her community as she hosts prayer initiatives, home groups, and individual prayer and counseling ministry.

195

Laurie founded Coffee House Parenting, LLC, and wrote her first book, *Coffee House Parenting,* where she shares from the heart practical means to pour your faith back into your families while making time to connect with God.

In this book, *Seeing Through the Darkness,* Laurie shares candidly about her journey of losing her vision in one eye and how the broken pieces of her faith lay before her—pieces she would find in the darkness that now enabled her to see.

LAURIEDEVERNOE.COM

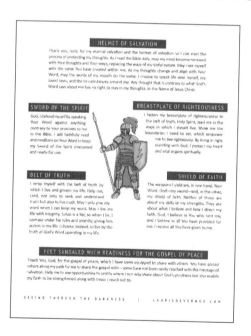

PUT ON THE FULL ARMOR OF GOD EVERY DAY!

For your FREE download with a prayer for each piece of armor visit www.lauriedevernoe.com/subscribe.

Made in the USA
Middletown, DE
23 August 2024

59079298R00119